日英対訳

BUSHIDO
THE SOUL OF JAPAN

新渡戸稲造=著

増澤史子=英語解説

IBCパブリッシング

装　　幀 = 岩目地英樹（コムデザイン）

英語解説 = 増澤史子

翻　　訳 = 澤田組

ナレーション ＝ ハワード・コルフィールド

本書は、2012年に弊社から刊行された『対訳ライブラリー 英語で読む武士道』を再編集したものです。

目　次

はじめに —— 武士道の英語

　「願わくはわれ太平洋の橋とならん」は *Bushido, The Soul of Japan* の作者、新渡戸稲造の有名なことばです。その新渡戸が病気療養のために米国のカリフォルニア州に滞在している間に執筆したのが『武士道』です。1899年、38歳のときでした。20歳前半で米国に留学し、30歳で結婚した相手もアメリカ人であり、また彼は、敬虔なクエーカー教徒でもありました。新渡戸稲造のバックグランドを知っておくと、この『武士道』を理解するのに、役立つのではないでしょうか。

　海外に行くと、必ず「日本人とは何か」ということに直面します。意外に、身近な質問から問題意識が出て、掘り下げていくようになることが多いものです。

　新渡戸自身も『武士道』を執筆する際に、妻からの「なぜ、日本人は……」の度重なる質問に対して、いかに満足のいく回答をしようかと考えているうちに、武士道を語らずして日本人の倫理観は語れないという結論になったと述べています。

　『武士道』が海外で多く読まれている理由は、英語で発信されたことと、出版当時、日本がロシアを相手に日露戦争に勝利をおさめたので、かくも小さき国に住む人々が大国ロシアに勝った「不思議」を解明するために多く読まれたということがあります。

　3.11の東日本大震災の未曾有の危機の中、粛々としてとった日本人の態度に世界から多くの賞賛が寄せられましたが、その際も海外のマスコミはこの日本人の態度を説明するのに『武士道』を引用していました。

この本は新渡戸が実際に書いた英語を現代語にしてわかり
やすくしたものですが、格調が高く、どの文をとっても深い味
わいが感じられます。

　グローバル化が叫ばれている今、グローバルな人材の条件と
は何かと問われれば、いくつか挙げられますが、その一つに欠
かせないのが自分のidentityではないしょうか。世界に日本人
の底に流れる宗教観、倫理観、価値観を説明するのにこの本は
きっと役に立つと思われます。何よりも、日本人の教養として
『武士道』はおさえておく必要があるでしょう。

　本の最後のパラグラフ、"Like its symbolic flower, after it
is blown in all directions by the winds, Bushido will still
bless mankind with its perfume. It will enrich life. Long
after; when its practices have been buried and its very
name forgotten, its aroma will come floating in the air; as
from a distant, unseen hill." に至る新渡戸の考え方を学んで
みてはいかがでしょうか。

2012年 初夏

増澤　史子

本書の構成

本書は、

　　　□読みはじめる前に
　　　□英日対訳による本文
　　　□欄外の語注
　　　□各章ごとの役立つ英語表現
　　　□MP3形式の英文音声

で構成されています。本書は、欧米のビジネス界でも高く評価されている
「武士道」についてのストーリーを、英語／日本語で読み進めながら、同時
にいろいろなシーンで役立つ英語表現の習得にも活用していただこうと
するものです。

　各ページの下部には、英語を読み進める上で助けとなるよう単語・熟語
の意味が掲載されています。また左右ページは、段落のはじまりが対応し
ていますので、日本語を読んで英語を確認するという読み方もスムーズに
できるようになっています。また各章末にはビジネス英語の権威で数多く
の著書を執筆されている増澤史子昭和女子大教授による英語解説があり
ますので、本文を楽しんだ後に、英語の使い方などをチェックしていただ
くのに最適です。

　添付のCD-ROMには、MP3形式の音声が収録されています。お好きな
携帯プレーヤーに、お好きな箇所をダウンロードして繰り返し聞いていた
だくことで、発音のチェックだけでなく、英語で物語を理解する力が自然
に身に付きます。

Bushido
The Soul of Japan

武士道

Preface

I was often asked by my wife and other people why certain ideas and customs existed in Japan. In particular, one European man was surprised that religion is not taught in the schools in Japan. He wondered how moral education was taught. I thought about my own ideas of right and wrong. I came to realize that my "teacher" was Bushido and that I could not explain the customs to my wife and others if they did not understand feudalism and Bushido. With this in mind, I wrote this book.

I use examples from European history and literature in order to aid the understanding of foreign readers. I believe deeply in the teachings of Christ, but I do not like the later methods and forms which darken those teachings. I also believe in the law written in the hearts of all people in all nations. I am well instructed in things new and old both in Japan and the rest of the world. I include foreign impressions of Japan—good and bad.

This book is more than an important message to the rest of the world. It helps in solving one of the biggest problems of our time—the unity of East and West.

■moral education 徳育　■come to realize ～に気づく　■customs 图慣習
■feudalism 图封建制度　■in order to ～するために　■unity 統一、結束

序　文

　妻*や周囲の人たちから日本に存在する考えや慣習についてよく質問を受けた。中でも、あるヨーロッパの男性は日本の学校で宗教を教えないことに驚いていた。ではどうやって道徳教育をするのかという。私は自分自身の善悪の観念について考えた。すると自分の「教師」は武士道であり、封建制と武士道を理解してもらわなければその慣習も説明できないと気がついた。それを念頭において、この本を書いた。

　ヨーロッパの歴史や文学も例にしたので外国の読者にも理解しやすくなっている。私はキリストの教えを深く信じているが、その教えを暗くする最近の方式は好きではない。私はまた世界中の国々のあらゆる人々の心に刻まれた律法も信じている。日本や諸外国における新旧の物事についてはよく教えを受けてきた。外国から見た日本に対する印象を、良い点も悪い点も盛りこんだ。

　この本は諸外国に向けた大切なメッセージというだけではない。東西の結束というこの時代における最大の問題を解決する一助である。

＊**妻**　新渡戸の妻メリーのこと。新渡戸はアメリカ留学中、クエーカー派の集会でアメリカ人メリー・エルキントン（1857-1938）と出会い、1891年に結婚した。

Part I
Chapter 1 – Chapter 5

Chapter 1

Bushido as an Ethical System

Chivalry is as much a part of Japan as its national flower, the cherry blossom. It is not an old, dry, historical virtue. It is still a living object of power and beauty. While it has no shape, we know that we are under its influence. The social conditions in which it was born have long disappeared. The light of chivalry, which was a child of feudalism, still shines upon us with its moral teaching. It is a pleasure for me to think about it, as it is for some English people to think about their past knights in shining armor. It is sad and disappointing to note, however, that even some scholars do not know that chivalry ever existed anywhere at any time. Carl Marx, in his *Capital*, however, urged his readers to study the social and political institutions of feudalism, as it then existed in Japan. I also hope my readers will study the chivalry of present day Japan.

■ethical 形道徳上の　■chivalry 名騎士道 (精神)　■virtue 名美徳、美点
■armor 名よろい、甲冑　■urge 動強く勧める　■institution 名制度

第1章

道徳体系としての武士道

　武士道は日本の国花である桜と同じように大切なものである。古ぼけてひからびた歴史上の美徳ではない。今なお息づく力と美の象徴である。形はなくても、周知のように私たちはその影響を受けている。武士道が生まれた社会状況は消えて久しい。それでも封建制から生まれた武士道の光は、その道徳の教えによっていまだに私たちを照らしている。武士道について考えるのは喜ばしいことである。イギリス人の中には光り輝く鎧に身をつつんだ昔の騎士のことを考えるのが好きな人もいるだろう、それと同じだ。武士道がかつて世界に存在していたことすら知らない学者がいるのは嘆かわしい。しかしカール・マルクス＊は著書『資本論』で、封建制の社会的政治制度は日本に存在したと述べており、その研究をするよう読者に勧めている。本書の読者にも現代の日本における武士道を勉強してほしいと思う。

＊**カール・マルクス**（1818-1883）　ドイツの経済学者、哲学者、革命家。『資本論』『共産党宣言』などが有名。

I do not intend to compare European and Japanese feudalism. My attempt is rather to write about the origin and sources of our chivalry, its character and teaching. I also write about its influence on the masses and the continuing permanence of that influence.

The Japanese word which I have roughly called chivalry is more than just horsemanship. Bu-shi-do literally means Military-Knight-Ways. These are the ways which fighting nobles should observe in their daily lives and follow in their work. They are the moral rules of the warrior class. From now on I would like to use the Japanese word because it is a teaching which is very unique and produces a distinct type of mind and character. So it is with some words. They are very expressive of national character. This is not just the case with some Japanese words but also other languages.

Bushido, then, is a set of moral rules which the samurai had to follow. It is an unspoken law written only in the heart of man. It was founded not by one man alone but was the result of the natural growth of centuries of military careers. Early in the 17th century there were military laws (*buke hatto*). They had to do mostly with marriages, castles and so on, almost nothing about moral instruction. We cannot, therefore, point to a definite time and say, "Here is where it began." It was born in the feudal age but feudalism itself is hard to identify with a specific time.

■attempt 图試み、企て　■permanence 图永続（性）　■observe 動順守する
■distinct 形独特な　■expressive 形〜を表現する　■moral rule 道徳規則
■moral instruction 道徳教育

ヨーロッパと日本の封建制を比べるつもりはない。私が書こうとしているのはむしろ武士道がどこからどう始まったか、その性質と教えについて、そして民衆への影響とそれがどこまで永続していくかについてである。

　私が英語でChivalryと書いている言葉は、日本語では騎士道以上の意味を持つ。「武士道」という語は戦う騎士の道を意味する。戦いをする高潔な人間が日々の生活、仕事をする上で従うべき道であり、武士階級のための道徳規則である。これより先、原語の「武士道」という言葉をそのまま使わせていただくが、それは武士道が他に類のない教えであり、独特な精神と性質を生み出しているからである。そうした特質を持つ言葉は他にもある。国民的な性質を非常によくあらわした言葉だ。これは日本語だけにとどまらず、他の言語でも同じである。

　武士道は、侍が従うよう定められた道徳上の規則である。これは暗黙の了解であり、心のうちにだけ刻まれていた。特定の誰かが作ったのではなく、武士の世が栄えるに従って生み出された成果である。17世紀初頭には武家諸法度という法令があったが、結婚、城などに関する規律が主で、道徳についてはほとんど触れられていなかった。従って、特定の時期を指して「ここから始まった」と言うのは不可能だ。封建時代に始まってはいるものの、封建制そのものについても時期を確定するのは難しい。

In England the political institutions of feudalism may be said to date from the Norman Conquest (1066). In Japan we may also say that its rise was at the same time Yoritomo came to power in the 12th century. But in England we find that the social elements of feudalism go back to the period previous to William the Conqueror. The seeds of feudalism in Japan also existed long before Yoritomo.

Also, in Japan as in Europe, when feudalism formally started, the professional class of warriors naturally became widely known. These were known as samurai, meaning guards or attendants.

The Sino-Japanese word *buke* or *bushi* came into common use in Japan. The words mean "fighting knights," who were a privileged class. Originally they must have been a rough breed whose work was fighting. They were selected in a natural way. Only the strongest survived over periods of constant war. To borrow Emerson's phrase, they were "a rude race, all masculine, with brutish strength." They had many advantages, great honor and heavy responsibility. Soon they felt the need of a common standard of behavior, especially since they were always fighting and belonged to different clans. They were in need of some measure by which to be judged such as fair play in fight, a primitive sense of childhood morality. Is this not the root of all military and civic virtue? The British boy had two ideals: 1) never bully a smaller boy and 2) never run away from a bigger one. This is the basis on which very strong morals can be built. This is

■come to power 権力を握る　■attendant 图付き人、従者　■Sino-Japanese 形中国日本間の　■privileged 形特権を持つ　■rough breed 粗野な生まれ　■masculine 形男っぽい　■brutish 形粗野な　■clan 图一族

イギリスでは封建制の政治制度が1066年のノルマン征服*から始まったともいわれる。日本でも12世紀に源頼朝が権力を握った頃に始まったと言ってよいかもしれない。しかしイギリスにおいては封建制の社会的要素は征服王ウィリアムⅠ世*までさかのぼる。日本でも封建制は頼朝の時代よりはるか昔に芽生えていた。

　また、これもヨーロッパ同様、日本でも封建制が正式に始まると、戦いを専門とする武士階級が広く知られるようになっていった。この階級が侍であり、侍という言葉には仕える者という意味がある。
　中国語に由来する言葉の「武家」、「武士」は日本で広く使われるようになった。どちらも、「戦う騎士」を意味し、特権階級に属する者を指したが、元々は戦いを仕事とする粗野な生まれの者たちであった。この特権階級は自然な形で選抜されていった。一番強いものだけが戦乱の世を生き延びたのだ。思想家エマソン*の言葉を借りれば、「荒っぽい人種で、みな力強く、獣のような強さ」を持つ者たちである。名誉もあれば責任も重く、さまざまな点で優位な立場にあった。まもなく彼らは共通の行動規範が必要だと感じるようになった。それというのもいつも戦っていた上、氏族もそれぞれ違ったからである。戦いにおけるフェアプレー精神、幼少期の素朴な道徳観のような何らかの基準を定める必要があった。これは武士も一般の民衆も含めたすべての人々の美徳に根ざすものではないだろうか？　イギリスの少年には２つの規範があった。１、自分より小さい子を絶対にいじめない。２、自分より大きい子から絶対に逃げ出さない。これは強い道徳心をつくる原

***ノルマン征服**　1066年、ノルマン人のノルマンディー公ギョーム（ウィリアムⅠ世）によるイングランド征服。
***ウィリアムⅠ世**（1027-1087）　イングランド王。ウィリアム征服王は通称。イングランドを征服し、ノルマン朝を開いて、イギリス王室の開祖となった。
***ラルフ・ウォルド・エマソン**（1803-1882）　アメリカの思想家、哲学者、詩人。

the basis on which the greatness of England was built. The same was true of Bushido.

Some of the most gentle-hearted of men also believe in war. For others it is the foundation of all the arts, high virtues and powers of men; war nourishes the great nations. Childhood begins with these ideas and so does knighthood, but this faith seeks its own justification, satisfaction and development. War without high moral support would fall far short of the ideals of knighthood and the samurai. One man said that religion, war and glory were the three souls of a perfect Christian knight. In Japan there were several sources of Bushido.

■nourish 動 ～を育てる　■faith 名 信念、信条　■seek 動 求める　■moral support 精神的支援　■fall short of 及ばない

則だ。偉大なイギリスが生んだ原則である。武士道にも同じことが言える。

　人々はこの上ない温和な心を持ちながら戦いを信じてもいる。別の視点からみればそれは芸術、高徳と力、すべての礎である。戦争は偉大な国家を育てる。少年期にはこうした考えを抱いていくもので、騎士道もそれは同じだが、この信条そのものを正当化し、充足し、発展させていかねばならない。道徳心を高く持たない戦争は騎士道や侍の理想からかけ離れてしまう。完全なるキリスト教徒の騎士は信仰、戦争、栄誉という3つの魂を持っている、とある人が言っているが、日本においても武士道にはいくつかの源があった。

Chapter 2

Sources of Bushido

One may begin with Buddhism, from which we get a sense of calm trust in Fate, a giving in to what will be. We have no fear of danger, bad luck or death. When a pupil equals his master, Zen Buddhism becomes the teacher. Zen leads one to reach levels of thought beyond words. Its method is long, quiet, deep thinking. It brings one to the realization of the basic Truth which underlies everything. Its goal is to be in harmony with that Truth. One awakens to a new heaven and a new earth.

■fate 名運命 ■give in 従う、譲歩する ■pupil 名弟子 ■underlie 動 〜の根底にある ■awaken 動目覚める

第2章

武士道の源

　武士道の源について、まずは仏教から始めたいと思う。仏教が武士道にもたらしたのは、これから起こることに身をまかせ、平静に運命の神に信をゆだねる感覚である。危険や悪運、死を恐れることもない。弟子が師匠からすべてを学んでしまうと、後は禅宗が師となる。禅によって思考は言葉を超えた領域に達する。その方法は長く静かに深く考えることだ。するとすべてのものに潜む基本的な真理を理解できるようになる。最終的に目指すのは真理との調和である。新しい天と新しい地に目覚めるのだ。

What we could not get from Buddhism was provided by Shinto abundantly—loyalty to the Emperor, respect for one's ancestors and devotion to one's parents. These things balanced the arrogance of the samurai with humility. Shinto teaches that man is basically good and pure. The mirror in a Shinto shrine is for you to see yourself, the very image of the Deity. It is for you to know yourself—your moral nature. Also, the nature-worship of Shinto makes our country dear to our souls. Ancestor-worship makes the Imperial family the fountainhead of the whole nation. To us the country is more than just soil for planting. It is the holy home of the gods. To us the Emperor is the bodily representative of Heaven on earth. It is said that British royalty is not only the image of authority but also the symbol of national unity. I believe that royalty in Japan is even stronger.

The teachings of Shinto have to do with the two main points of the emotional life of the Japanese people—love of country and loyalty. Our national faith is not based on philosophy or religion but on instinctive racial feelings. These strong and deep racial emotions were totally implanted in Bushido, not so much as teachings but as impulses. Shinto therefore provided rules for doing rather than believing.

■abundantly 副豊富に　■devotion 名献身　■arrogance 名尊大、傲慢
■humility 名謙虚　■deity 名神　■fountainhead 名根源　■instinctive 形本能的
な　■implant 動植え付ける

仏教で得られなかった部分は神道が存分に補ってくれた。天皇への忠誠、祖先に対する敬意、両親に対する献身である。これらは侍の傲慢さと謙虚さとをうまく調和させた。神道の教えでは人は基本的に善であり純粋である。神社に置かれている鏡は己を見つめるためのものであり、神の真の姿を映し出す。その鏡で自分自身を見つめ、己の精神的な姿を知るのである。また、神道の自然崇拝により、私たちの魂にとって国が大切な存在になる。祖先を崇めることで皇室が国家全体の源泉となる。国は私たちにとって単なる種をまく土地という以上に、神々の神聖な住みかである。天皇は地上において天をそのまま象徴している。イギリス王室は権力の象徴のみならず国家統一のシンボルとも言われている。日本の皇室はそれよりもっと強大なのではないだろうか。

　神道の教えは日本人の情緒的な特質である愛国心と忠誠心に通じている。国民的な信仰は哲学や宗教ではなく本能的な民族感情に基づくものだ。この強く深い民族感情は武士道に教えとしてではなく、衝動としてそっくり植えつけられている。ゆえに神道は信仰面よりも行動面においての規範を定めることとなった。

In regard to ethical instruction, the teachings of Confucius were much used for forming Bushido. The five moral relations—between master and servant (lord and follower), father and son, husband and wife, older and younger brother, friend and friend—were what Japanese racial instinct already knew. These ideas were well suited to the samurai, who formed the ruling class. In addition to Confucius, Mencius also had great influence on Bushido, even though some of his democratic theories were considered to be against the existing social order. Their writings formed the main textbooks for young people and were the highest authority in discussions among old people.

For the typical samurai, however, to have knowledge only was to be a fool. Book learning alone was compared to a bad-smelling vegetable that must be boiled and boiled before it can be used. Too little learning and too much learning were both unpleasant. The samurai thought that knowledge really becomes knowledge only when it is made a part of the mind of the learner and shows in his character. Intellect itself was therefore considered inferior to ethical emotion. Man and the universe both were thought to be spiritual and ethical. Bushido could not accept the judgment of Huxley—that the natural process was unmoral.

■in regard to ～に関して　■servant 名家来　■instinct 名本能　■well suited to ～
によく適している　■democratic 形民主主義の　■be inferior to ～より劣っている
■unmoral 形道徳に関係のない

倫理観に関しては、孔子の教えが武士道の形成のために多く用いられた。君臣、父子、夫婦、長幼、朋友という道徳における5つの関係（五倫）について、日本人は民族的な本能ですでに悟っていた。この教えは支配階級である侍に好都合だった。孔子*に加えて孟子*も武士道に少なくない影響を与えたが、その民本主義には従来の社会秩序に反する点もあると考えられていた。二人の著作は若者にとっては一番の教科書となり、大人には議論をかわすときの最高の権威を持つ書物となった。

　それでも典型的なある侍にとって、知識だけしか持たないのは愚かなことだった。書物で学ぶだけというのは何度も煮なければ食べられない臭い野菜にたとえられた。全然学ばないのも、学びすぎるのもよろしくない。その侍は知識が学ぶ者の心の一部となり、その人となりにあらわれて初めて真の知識となると考えた。そのため知性そのものは道徳感情より劣るとされた。人と宇宙どちらも精神的、道徳的なものであると考えられた。武士道は、ハクスリー*の唱えた宇宙の進行には道徳性がないという説とは相いれぬものであった。

*孔子（前551–前479）　中国の春秋時代の思想家。その教えは儒教へと発展し、日本など東アジア諸国に大きな影響をもたらした。

*孟子（前372–前289）　中国の戦国時代の儒学者。性善説を説き、仁義による王道政治を目指した。

*トマス・ヘンリー・ハクスリー（1825–1895）　イギリスの生物学者。ダーウィンの進化論を擁護した。

Knowledge, therefore, was not an end in itself but only a means to attaining wisdom. So anyone who stopped short of this goal was regarded as being nothing more than a machine. The true importance of knowledge was its **practical** application in life. This was repeated over and over by the Chinese philosopher Wan Yang Ming: "To know and to act are one and the same." Some of the noblest of *bushi* were strongly influenced by him. His writings have many similarities to those in the New Testament. "Seek first the kingdom of God and his righteousness; and all these things shall be given to you." This is a thought that may be found on almost any page of Wan Yang Ming. A Japanese disciple of his said that the lord of heaven and earth lives in the heart of man (his *kokoro*, mind). He is living and always shining. We know right and wrong by this, called conscience, which does not make errors. The Japanese mind, as expressed by the ideals of Shinto, was able to understand and appreciate Yang Ming's thoughts easily.

So the thoughts from various sources comprising Bushido were few and simple. They made possible the safe conduct of life through the unsafest periods in our history. By these thoughts a new and unique type of man was formed. In the 16th century everything was confused in Japan. But there was the need for each man to do justice for himself. Those conditions made man into a superb animal—totally militant.

■attain 動手に入れる　■wisdom 名知恵、英知　■application 名適用、応用
■righteousness 名正しさ　■disciple 名弟子　■conscience 名良心　■conduct 名
行為、運営　■militant 名闘士

従って、知識はただ知ればいいというものではなく、そこから知恵を身につけるための手段でしかなかった。だから誰でもそこまで到達できなければただの機械と同じだとみなされた。知識の真に大切な点は人生に実際に役立つようにすることである。中国の思想家の王陽明*はこれを「知行合一」としてくり返し説いた。彼の影響を受けた中には高潔な武士もいた。王陽明の著作には新約聖書に通じる点が数多くある。「何よりもまず、神の国と神の義とを求めなさい。そうすれば、これらのものはみな与えられるであろう」。これは王陽明の書のどのページでもほぼ目にする観念である。日本人の陽明学者は言った。「天と地の神は人の心の中にある。心の中で神は生き、輝いている。私たちはこれによって善悪の判断を知る。これは間違いをおかすことのない良心である」。日本人の心は、神道の理念にあらわれているとおり、陽明の考えをたやすく理解し認めることが可能だった。

　このように武士道の源となる思想は数も少なく単純であったが、そのおかげで歴史上のもっとも危険極まりない時代に生活を安全に導くことができた。これらの思想が今までにない独自の気風を持つ人間たちを作り出した。16世紀の日本はすべてが混迷していた。しかし個々の人間が自分自身のために正しい行いをすることが求められていた。こうした状況によって人はよりすぐれた動物、つまり完全なる闘士となった。

* **王陽明**（1472-1528）　中国の明代の儒学者。知行合一を主張し、陽明学を起こした。

Chapter 3

Correct Judgment or Justice

Here we clarify the strongest rule in the belief of the samurai. He hated most of all anything dishonest. He was ready to decide upon one kind of action or another in accordance with reason without hesitating. Die when it is right to die, fight when it is right to fight. His belief was like the bones which support the flesh and various parts of the body. Without bones one cannot be a human being. Without such a belief one could not be a samurai. Virtuous action, according to Mencius, is a straight and narrow path. Man ought to take it to regain the lost paradise.

Any name meaning mastery of learning or art was inferior to the name *Gishi* (righteous man). The famous 47 Samurai (of *Chūshingura*) are commonly known as the 47 *Gishi*.

■dishonest 形不正直な、不正の ■in accordance with ～に従って ■hesitate 動
ためらう ■flesh 名（動物の）肉 ■virtuous 形高潔な ■regain 動～を取り戻す
■lost paradise 失われた楽園 ■righteous 形公正な、高潔な

第3章

正しい判断、または正義

　ここで侍の信条でもっとも大切な規則を明確にする。侍は何よりも不誠実さを嫌った。侍はその時々に応じた行動を道理に従ってためらわずに決断する心構えができていた。死ぬべき時に死に、戦うべき時に戦う。侍の信条は体を支える骨に等しかった。骨がなくては人間ではありえない。このような信条がなくしては侍にはなれなかった。孟子のいう高潔な行動とは、正道を行くことだ。人はその道を進んで失われた楽園を取り戻さねばならない。

　知識や芸術に精通していかなる名声を得ても「義士」（節義をかたく守る人）の名声にはかなわなかった。忠臣蔵の有名な四十七人の侍は「四十七士」*として広く知られている。

*四十七人の忠臣　赤穂浪士のこと。元禄15年12月14日、元赤穂藩士大石内蔵助をはじめとする四十七人の浪人が、元主君であった播磨赤穂藩藩主浅野長矩（あさのながのり）の仇である吉良上野介の屋敷に討ち入りし仇討ちをした。

In times when cheating and lies were seen so much, this manly virtue, open and honest, was a jewel without parallel. It was the twin brother of bravery in battle.

Another word which may have derived from *Gi* is *Gi-ri*, which means right reason but which came to mean a sense of duty. Originally it meant the *Giri* we owe to parents, superiors, inferiors, society, etc. Love (of parents) should be the only reason for such a feeling. If there is no love (in some other relationship), man's reason must be the force which makes him behave in a righteous way. The same is true of any other moral obligation. As a reason for doing something, it is very much inferior to the Christian idea of love. I think it is the product of an unnatural society in which birth determines class differences, in which age (seniority) is considered more important than superior ability and so on. Because of this kind of unnatural society, *Giri* was used to call something evil "right"—for example, a daughter had to sell her body (virginity) in order to get money to pay for her father's bad habits. Starting as Right Reason, *Giri*, in time, became something completely different—a misleading, incorrect word (a monster)! It was used to pretend to be right. It could have been the tool of cowards. But Bushido had a keen and correct sense of courage—the spirit of daring and how one conducts himself in all situations.

(◎

■bravery 名勇敢さ　■derive from ～に由来する　■sense of duty 義務感、義理
■obligation 名義務(感)、責任　■seniority 名年功序列　■evil 形道義に反する
■daring 形大胆な　■conduct 動導く、行う

不正や嘘が横行した時代には、率直と誠実というこの雄々しい美徳は比類なき宝であり、戦いの場においては勇敢さと対をなすものだった。

　「義」に由来したと思われる言葉に「義理」もある。正しい道理という意味だが、義務感も意味するようになった。本来、義理とは両親や目上の者、目下の者、社会などに対し何かをする義務があることを示した。このような感覚を抱く理由があるとすればそれは両親の愛情だけだ。それ以外の関係においては、愛情がない場合、人が正しい道にそった行いをするには理性の力が必要となるだろう。他の道義的責任も同じである。何かする上での理由としては、キリスト教の愛の観念よりずいぶん劣る。生まれによって階級が分かれ、年功序列が才能の優劣より重んじられる不自然な社会が義理の感覚を生み出したのだろう。このような不自然な社会のせいで、よからぬ「正義」に対しても義理が使われることがあった。たとえば、ある娘が自分の貞操を売って父親の悪癖のつけを払わねばならなくなった場合などである。最初は「正しい道理」であった「義理」は、時が経つとまったく違うものへと変わり、怪物のようにまぎらわしく誤った言葉になってしまった。義理は正しいふりをするために使われた。卑怯者の手先にもなりえた。しかし武士道には強く正しい勇敢な心があった、それは豪胆、そしてすべての状況での振る舞い方を定める精神である。

Chapter 4

Courage, the Spirit of Daring and Bearing

To be daring means to be bold (fearless). One's bearing is how you conduct yourself in all situations (in peace, in danger, etc). Courage was not considered to be a virtue unless it was for Righteousness. Courage meant doing what is right. But to face danger or risk, or to die for something which is not right is foolishness, not courage. Anyone can die like a dog but true courage is to live when it is right to live and to die only when it is right to die.

■bearing 图 辛抱、我慢　■bold 形 大胆な、力強い　■die like a dog 犬死する

第4章

勇気 ── 豪胆と忍耐の精神

　豪胆とは恐れを知らない、勇敢という意味だ。忍耐とは平和なとき
や危機的状況など、すべての状況における振る舞い方である。勇気が
あっても道義的に正しくなければ美徳とはみなされない。勇気という
のは正しい行いをすることだった。危険に直面したときや正義以外の
ために死ぬのは愚かな行為であり、勇気ではない。誰でも犬死はでき
るが、真の勇気とは生きるべきときに生き、死ぬべきときにのみ死ぬ
ことである。

A truly brave man is always calm, serene. He is never taken by surprise, even in the face of death. He is cool in battle, unshaken by earthquakes and laughs at storms. In extreme danger he can write a poem, sing a song quietly to himself. These are the signs of a big spirit, a mind capable of holding much (*yoyū*). Things which are serious to ordinary people are simply play to the brave man. He is ready to exchange witty remarks with the enemy. If the enemy is brave, he will not be put to shame by the conquering warrior. The enemy could be respected and even loved. During the Sengoku period (about 1500) two famous feudal lords had been fighting each other for 14 years—Uesugi Kenshin of the Niigata area and Takeda Shingen of the Yamanashi area. When Kenshin heard of Shingen's death, he cried aloud at the loss of "the best of enemies." It was this same Kenshin who had set a noble example for all time in his treatment of Shingen. Shingen's area was away from the sea and he could not get salt from the sea or from another area whose lord had refused to supply him with it. When Kenshin heard about Shingen's problem, he decided to supply him with salt, even though they were at war. Kenshin said, "I do not fight with salt but with the sword." Bravery and honor alike require that we should have as enemies only those who are worthy of being friends in peace.

■serene 形穏やかな、憂いのない　■be taken by surprise 不意をつかれる　■capable 形能力がある　■witty 形機知に富んだ　■put to shame 惨めな負け方をする　■those who ～する人々　■worthy 形～するに値する

真に勇敢な人間はつねに冷静沈着である。死を目前にしても度を失ったりしない。戦いにあっても落ちつきはらい、地震にも揺るがず嵐をも笑い飛ばす。危険きわまりない中でも詩が書けるし、静かに一人で歌を吟じることもできる。これらは傑出した精神のしるしであり、精神に余裕があることを示す。凡人には深刻な事態も勇敢な人間にとっては単なる遊びである。敵と気のきいたやり取りをかわす余裕がある。相手の武士が勇敢な敵であれば、倒して恥をかくことはない。敵であろうと尊敬されもすれば愛されもする。戦国時代(1500年頃)、二人の有名な武将が14年にわたって戦い続けた。越後(新潟)の上杉謙信と甲斐(山梨)の武田信玄である。信玄の死を耳にした謙信は、「最良の敵」を失い、声をあげて泣いた。この謙信こそが信玄に対する扱いにおいてつねに高潔な見本を示した人物だった。信玄の土地は海から遠く離れていたため、他の土地の武将に拒まれると塩を手に入れることができなくなった。謙信はその話を聞き、戦いの最中だったにも関わらず塩を送った。謙信いわく、「私は塩ではなく、剣で戦う」。勇敢も名誉も、平和なときに友となる価値のある人間のみを敵とすべしと要求する。

Strength of mind and body and fearless courage appeal very much to young minds. They are the qualities that young boys wanted to imitate and have as their own. Stories of military courage were well known from a very early age. A mother would become angry at her little boy if he complained about some small pain. She would say, "What will you do when your arm is cut off in battle? What will you do if you have to do *hara-kiri*?" Even when his stomach is empty, for a samurai it is a disgrace to show that he is hungry. Many such stories are told but they are not the only way of building a daring and fearless spirit. Sometimes a samurai's son was not given food, or was made to go out in the cold to test his endurance. Very young children were made to rise before the sun, to study before breakfast, to walk to their teacher's place with bare feet in the middle of winter, or to stay up all night without sleep.

Does this ultra-Spartan way of training the nerves shock the modern educator? Do you think these things bruised the tender emotions of the young heart? Let us see in another chapter what other concepts Bushido had of valor.

■disgrace 图不名誉 ■be made to do ～させられる、～する羽目になる
■endurance 图忍耐力 ■bare feet はだし ■bruise 動～を傷つける ■tender 形
優しい、感じやすい ■valor 图勇敢さ

精神と肉体の強さ、恐れを知らぬ勇気の力は若者の心に大きく訴え
かける。青年が見習い、自分なりに身につけたいと願う素質だ。子ども
たちはほんの小さな頃から武功話を聞かされていた。母親はわずかな
痛みで駄々をこねる幼い息子を叱ったりした。母親は言う。「戦いで腕
を切り落とされたらどうするのですか。切腹しなければいけなくなっ
たらどうするのですか」。たとえ腹ぺこであっても、侍が空腹なありさ
まを見せるのは面目ないことである。こうした話はいくつも語られて
いるが、これだけが恐れを知らぬ豪胆な精神を築く道ではない。時に
は侍の子が食事を与えられなかったり、忍耐力を試すために寒さの中
に放り出されたりした。年端のいかぬ子たちが日の出前に起こされて、
朝食前に勉強するため冬のさなかに先生の家まで裸足で歩いて行かさ
れたり、一睡もせず徹夜させられたりもした。

　こうした超スパルタ式*の精神修養は現代の教育者に衝撃を与える
だろうか？　このようなやり方は幼い心の優しい情緒に傷あとを残し
ただろうか？　武士道における勇猛さの他の面については次の章で見
ていくことにしよう。

---

*スパルタ式　元々は、古代ギリシアのポリス・スパルタで行われていた教育方式を指す。丸刈り、裸で鍛えら
れ、障害が生じた子どもを殺していく厳しい教育方式であり、これが転じて、日本では「スパルタ教育」「スパ
ルタ式」といって厳しい教育を指すようになった。

Chapter 5

Kindness, the Feeling of Mental Pain

Love, giving freely (money, time, etc.), the feeling of tenderness for another person, sympathy and pity have always been recognized as the highest virtues of the human soul. These are the virtues worthy of a prince. Many times both Confucius and Mencius said that the highest requirement of a ruler of men is to be kind and good. Confucius said that if a prince is kind, all the people will come to him willingly; with people will come land; land will bring wealth and those riches will be used in the right way. The virtue of kindness is the root and wealth is the fruit. If the ruler is kind, the people will love what is right. A ruler must win the hearts of the people.

■tenderness 名優しさ　■sympathy 名共感、同情　■pity 名哀れみ　■willingly 副
喜んで、進んで　■win the heart of（人）の心をつかむ

第5章

思いやり——痛みの感情

　愛情、金銭や時間などを惜しみなく与えること、他人に対する思いやりの気持ち、あわれみや同情はつねに人間の魂でいちばん高い美徳とされてきた。これらは君主にふさわしい美徳である。孔子や孟子もくり返し言っている。支配者にもっとも必要とされるのは思いやりと善なる心だ。孔子は君主に思いやりがあれば、人民は喜んで集まってくると言った。人が集まれば土地も集まる。土地は財産をもたらしその富は正しく使われる。思いやりの美徳が根源にあり、それが財産として実を結ぶ。支配者に思いやりがあれば、人々は正しい行いを愛するようになる。支配者は人々の心をつかまねばならない。

During the time of feudalism, which could have developed into morally low-level militarism, we were saved from unjust rule by good men. They were men who thought of themselves as the first servants of the State. Feudalism therefore did not produce unjust rulers. A feudal prince felt a high sense of duty to his ancestors and to heaven and was also a father to his subjects. Confucius taught that "when the prince loves what the people love, and hates what the people hate, then he is called the parent of the people." The ruler and the people become one.

So, in a way that we do not usually think of it, Bushido accepted and supported a fatherly type of government. It did not support that of a less interested uncle (like Uncle Sam!). The difference between an unjust and a fatherly government is that in the former case the people obey unwillingly; in the latter they obey freely, willingly and whole-heartedly. In some other countries the ruler has been called the king of devils because the princes were evil. Or he was called the king of asses because of never-ending taxes and other unjust practices. In still other countries, however, the ruler has been called the king of men because the people followed him willingly.

■unjust 形不正な、不当な ■state 名国家 ■subject 名臣下 ■fatherly 形父親らしい ■ass 名ロバ ■practice 名慣習、ならわし

封建制の時代は道徳心の低い武断政策に発展しかねなかったが、善なる心を持つ支配者のおかげで私たちは不当な支配から守られた。彼らは自分自身を国家の第一のしもべであるとみなしていた。ゆえに封建制が不当な支配者を生み出すことはなかった。封建制の君主は祖先や天に対して高い義務感を持ち、臣下に対しては父であった。孔子は「民の愛するものを愛し、民の憎むものを憎むとき、君主は民の父と呼ばれる」と説いた。支配者と民はこうして結ばれる。

　そういうわけで、私たちが普通は考えないようなやり方で武士道は父権主義の政府を認め、支持した。利害関係がもっと少ない叔父政治（米国にみられるような民主主義）は支持しなかった。不当な支配と父権政府の違いは、前者は人々が自分の意志に反して従うのに対し、後者は進んでみずからの意志により心から従っているという点である。他の国々においては、支配者は悪者だからと悪魔の王と呼ばれる。そうかと思えば際限ない課税やその他の不当な悪習のためにロバの王とも呼ばれる。その一方、さらに他の国では民が望んでついていくため人の王と呼ばれる。

Virtue and absolute power may strike the Western mind as being out of harmony. According to Bismarck, however, absolutism demands in the ruler fairness, honesty, devotion to duty, energy and inward humility. Another German leader spoke of "Kingship, by the grace of God, with its heavy duties, its great responsibility to God alone, from which no man or government can release the king."

Correct judgment and justice are considered to be father-like. But kindness, mercy and a gentle heart are thought to be tender and mother-like. We were warned against being too kind without the right amount of correct judgment and justice. One man said that excessive right judgment/justice is too hard and stiff and being too kind becomes a weakness. The bravest people are the most tender and loving people are daring people. *Bushi no nasake* (the tenderness of the warrior) appealed to that which is noble in us. It was not because the mercy of a samurai was different from the mercy of other people, but because it was a mercy which recognized due regard for justice. It was not just a state of mind but was backed with the power to save or kill.

■absolutism 名 絶対主義 ■fairness 名 公正、公平 ■honesty 名 正直、誠実
■inward 形 心の中の ■mercy 名 慈悲 ■excessive 形 過度の ■stiff 形 堅い、固い
■state of mind 心理状態

42　　Chapter 5　Kindness, the Feeling of Mental Pain

西洋人は美徳と絶対権力は調和しないという印象を持つかもしれない。だがビスマルクによれば、絶対主義には公正、誠実、義務への専心、活力と内なる謙虚さが要求される。別のドイツ人指導者はこう語っている。「王位は、神の恩寵によるものであり、神のみが担うその重い義務と大きな責任から、何びとといえども政府も王を解放することはできない」

　正しい判断と正義は父性的だとみなされる。しかし思いやり、慈悲、温和な心は優しく母性的なものだ。適切な正しい判断と正義なしにただ優しすぎるだけなのは戒められた。「義に過ぎれば固くなる。仁に過ぎれば弱くなる」という言葉がある。勇敢な人間はもっとも優しく、愛情あふれる人間は豪胆な人間だ。「武士の情け」は私たちの中の高潔な心に訴えかける優しさである。侍の情けが他の人々の慈悲と違うからではなくて、当然正義のためとみなされるからだ。単なる心の動きとは違い、人の生き死にを左右できる力に裏打ちされていたのである。

The samurai fully supported what Mencius taught concerning the power of love. "Kindness," he said, "influences anything which is in its way, just as water overcomes fire. The feeling of distress is the root of kindness, so a good man is always mindful of people who are suffering and in distress." These noble ideas are shared by various countries.

Kindness to the weak, the oppressed or the defeated was a virtue which was becoming to a samurai. Lovers of Japanese art must be familiar with the sight of a priest riding backwards on a cow. The rider was once a warrior who was equated with terror. In that terrible battle of Sumano-ura (1184 A.D.), he overtook one of the enemy and had hold of him in his gigantic arms. The etiquette of war at that time required that, on such occasions, the defeated should not be killed unless he was of equal rank or ability to the stronger one. The conquering warrior demanded the name of the other. But the weaker man made no sound. So his helmet was torn off, which revealed a young, beardless face. The very surprised knight relaxed his hold, helped the youth to his feet and ordered him to go. "Flee, young prince, to your mother's side! The sword of Kumagai will never be stained by your blood. Go, before your enemies come!" The young warrior refused to go and begged Kumagai (for the honor of both of them) to kill him on the spot. His sword had taken many lives before but now he hesitates—he can't do it. He has a vision of

■distress 图苦悩、苦痛　■suffer 動苦しむ　■terror 图恐怖　■overtake 動追い越す、上回る　■etiquette 图礼儀作法　■reveal 動明らかにする　■be stained by 〜で染まる　■on the spot すぐその場で

武士は孟子の説く仁愛の力を全面的に支持した。「思いやりは、出会うものすべてに影響を及ぼす。ちょうど水が火に打ち勝つのと同じだ。思いやりの根源にあるのは苦痛の感情で、善なる心を持つ人間はいつも苦痛に悩まされる人々を心に留めている」。こうした高潔な考えは他の国々でも共有されている。

　弱者や迫害された者、敗北者に対する思いやりは侍となるための美徳であった。日本画の愛好家なら僧が逆向きで牛に乗る絵をご存じだろう。乗っている僧はかつてその名を恐れられた武士、熊谷直実*だ。須磨の浦の激戦で彼は敵の一人に襲いかかり、巨大な腕で相手をねじ伏せた。当時の戦いの作法として、こういう場合には負かされた方が勝った方と対等の位にあるか、もしくは自分と同じ程度の能力を持つ者でなければ相手を殺すことはできなかった。勝った武士は相手に名乗るよう迫った。しかし負かされた方は何も言わなかった。そこで兜を脱がせてみると、まだ髭も生えぬ幼い顔があらわれた。熊谷は大変驚いて腕をゆるめ、若者に手を貸して立たせるとその場から去るようにと言った。「逃げなされ、若殿よ、母君の元へ！　熊谷の刃を殿の血に染めることはしない。行きなされ、敵が来る前に！」。若武者は行くのを拒み、お互いの名誉のため熊谷にそこで自分を殺すように頼んだ。その剣で彼はそれまでに多くの命を奪ってきたが、ここでためらいが生じて、相手を斬れない。自分の愛する息子がまさにこの日に初めて

---

*熊谷直実　（1141-1207）。平安時代末期から鎌倉時代初期の武士。『平家物語』に出てくる一の谷の戦いでの平敦盛との一騎打ちは有名。

his own beloved son who this very day went into battle. The strong hand of the warrior shakes. Again he begs the youth to flee for his life. The young man does not move and now one can hear the approaching steps of Kumagai's comrades. "If they find you, your fate will be worse than that by my hand. May the gods receive your soul." In an instant the sword flashes in the air and when it falls it is red with young blood. When the war is over, the conquering soldier returns but now, for him, honor and fame are not important. He gives up his military career, shaves his head, puts on the clothing of a priest, and devotes the remainder of his life to holy work.

This story shows that tenderness, pity and love were very much a part of the samurai's character, even at times of bloody encounters. An old saying among the samurai was that a bird hunter must not kill one which flies to his chest for protection. This does a lot to explain why the Red Cross movement, considered to be so Christian, was quickly and strongly accepted by us. Long before we ever heard of the Geneva Convention, Bakin, our greatest novelist, had taught us about medical treatment for a fallen enemy.

■beg 動懇願する ■comrade 名同僚、仲間 ■fame 名名声 ■devote 動ささげる
■fallen 形陥落した、壊滅した

戦いに加わった情景が脳裏によみがえる。たくましい手が震える。ふたたび熊谷は若武者に逃げて命を守るようにと言う。若武者は動かず、もう熊谷の仲間が近づく足音が聞こえてくる。「見つかったら、私の手にかかるより悪いことになる。後々菩提を弔いましょうぞ」。一瞬のうちに刃が空にきらめき、振り下ろされるや若武者の血で赤く染まった。戦いが終わり、熊谷は帰郷するものの、もう名誉も名声も重要ではなかった。そして武士としての経歴を捨て、頭を丸め僧衣をまとって残りの生涯を行脚にささげてしまう。

　この話は思いやりと慈悲と愛が侍の性質において非常に大切なものであり、血を流すような戦いの場にあってもそれは変わらないことを示している。侍の間に伝わる古いことわざに、猟師は助けを求めて懐に飛んできた鳥を殺してはならない（窮鳥懐に入れば猟師も殺さず）というものがあった。キリスト教の色がかなり濃いと考えられている赤十字の活動が急速に日本で根づいた理由は、このことわざによってかなり説明がつく。ジュネーヴ条約を耳にするよりかなり昔に、大作家の滝沢馬琴も倒れた敵に薬を与えて治す話を書いていた。

In Satsuma (the western part of Kagoshima), famous for its martial spirit and education, there was a custom among young men to practice music. It was the tender sound of the *biwa* which took their thoughts away from war. The same kind of custom existed in Arcadia (ancient Greece). It is said that due to the influence of music there was no cruelty in that part of the country. It was not only in Satsuma where gentleness was taught to the warrior class. A prince of Shirakawa advised us to cherish the fragrance of flowers, the sound of distant bells and the sounds of insects on a cold night. He also said that we should forgive the breeze that scatters your flowers, the cloud that hides your moon and someone who tries to fight with you.

The writing of poetry was encouraged not only to express these feelings but also to cultivate them. In our poetry, therefore, there is a strong undercurrent of pity and tenderness. The soul of the brave warrior could even be awakened to the sweet notes of the *uguisu*. Often a marching soldier would halt, take out writing utensils from his belt, and compose a poem. Such papers were found later in the helmets or breastplates of the lifeless writers. Compassion can be brought out in people in various ways. In Japan, among the hardened samurai, it was brought about by the love of music and poetry. This, in turn, brings out consideration for the feelings of others.

■martial spirit 勇敢な精神 ■due to ～に起因して ■cruelty 图 残虐な行為 ■cherish 動 ～を大事にする ■poetry 图 詩 ■undercurrent 图 底意 ■halt 動 立ち止まる ■utensil 图 用具 ■in turn 回りまわって

勇猛果敢と教育で有名な薩摩（鹿児島県西部）では、若者が音楽を稽古する習慣がある。琵琶の優しい音色が戦いから頭を引き離してくれる。同じような習慣が古代ギリシアのアルカディアにもあった。音楽のおかげでその地方には残虐行為が起こらなかったという。武士階級に風流なたしなみがあったのは薩摩だけではなかった。白河の君主は花の香り、遠くで聞こえる鐘の音、寒い夜の虫の音をいつくしむことと助言している。花を散らす風、月を隠す雲、戦いをいどんでくる者をも許すべきだとも言っている。

　このような感情を表現するだけでなく教養を磨くためにも詩作が勧められた。そのため日本人の創る詩の奥底には、強いあわれみと優しさが隠れている。勇敢な武士の魂はウグイスの甘い声にさえも呼びさまされる。行軍する武士が立ち止まり、帯から筆を出し、詩を作ることもよくあった。死者の兜や胸あての中からこうした書きつけが見つかった。同情の念をはぐくむ方法はいろいろある。日本では、荒ぶる武士にあっても、それは音楽と詩への愛を通じてはぐくまれる。そして、ひるがえって、音楽や詩を愛する心はまた他者を思いやる気持ちをはぐくむ。

役立つ英語表現 1

【observe】

These are the ways which fighting nobles should **observe** in their daily lives and follow in their work.（p.14, 7行目）
戦いをする高潔な人間が日々の生活、仕事をする上で従うべき道である。

動詞observe は「規則などを守る、規則に従う」という意味で用いられることが多いです。

All employees must observe a new company policy on smoking.
全社員は喫煙に関する社の新方針を厳守してください。

【identify】

Feudalism itself is hard to **identify** with a specific time.（p.14, 21行目）
封建制そのものについても時期を確定するのは難しい。

identifyという英語は日本語にしにくい英語の一つです。「あるものがそうだと確認する」ことです。身分証明書はIDと言いますがIdentification Cardのことです。

Identify the problem immediately.
すぐに問題をつきとめなさい。

【responsibility】

They had many advantages, great honor and heavy **responsibility**.
（p.16, 15行目）
名誉もあれば責任も重く、様々な点で優位な立場にあった。

responsibilityは「責任」という意味ですが、「責務」という意味で、仕事の範囲を表します。形容詞は responsible です。

> My responsibility is to do the inventory check.
> 私の仕事は在庫管理です。

> I'm responsible for a new project.
> 私は新しいプロジェクトの責任者です。

【measure】

> They were in need of some **measure** by which to be judged such as fair play in fight, a primitive sense of childhood morality. （p.16, 18行目）
> 戦いにおけるフェアプレー精神、幼少期の素朴な道徳観のような何らかの基準を定める必要があった。

measure はここでは「基準」という意味ですが、通常は「方法」や「手段」という意味で用いられています。

> We have to think about a temporary measure against the appreciation of the yen.
> 円高に対して臨時的措置を講じなくてはなりません。

【fall short of】

> War without high moral support would **fall** far **short of** the ideals of knighthood and the samurai. （p.18, 7行目）
> 道徳心を高く持たない戦争は騎士道や侍の理想からかけ離れてしまう。

fall short of は「～に足りない」という意味です。fall shy of という言い方もできます。

> The results of the oil company fell short of Wall Street expectations.
> その石油会社の業績はウォール街の期待に達しなかった。

【based on】

> Our national faith is not **based on** philosophy or religion but on instinctive racial feelings. (p.22, 17行目)
> 国民的な信仰は哲学や宗教ではなく本能的な民族感情に基づくものだ。

based on は「～に基づいて」という意味です。また based at London などというと「ロンドンに本拠（本店）を置く」という意味になります。

> Based on the market research, he made up his mind to open a bakery shop in Shibuya.
> 市場調査に基いて、彼は渋谷にベイカリー（パン屋）をオープンすることを決心した。

【in regard to】

> **In regard to** ethical instruction, the teachings of Confucius were much used for forming Bushido. (p.24, 1行目)
> 倫理観に関しては、孔子の教えが武士道の形成のために多く用いられた。

regard という単語はビジネスでは多くみかけます。ここでの in regard to は「～に関して」という意味です。with reference to も同様に使われます。

> In regard to the contract renewal, we have no objection.
> 契約の更新に関しては、当方は異存はありません。

【in accordance with】

> He was ready to decide upon one kind of action or another **in accordance with** reason without hesitating. (p.28, 2行目)
> 彼（侍）はその時々に応じた行動を道理に従ってためらわずに決断する心構えができていた。

in accordance with は、契約書では頻繁にでてくる表現で、「～に従って」という意味です。

It shall be settled in accordance with the arbitration rules.
仲裁規則に基いて解決される。

【seniority】

> I think it is the product of an unnatural society in which birth determines class differences, in which age (**seniority**) is considered more important than superior ability and so on. （p.30，11行目）
> 生まれによって階級が分かれ、年功序列が才能の優劣より重んじられる不自然な社会が義理の感覚を生み出したのだろう。

seniorityは「年功序列」のこと。seniority systemは「年功序列制度」のことです。一方、「能力主義」はmerit systemと呼ばれています。

Global players tend to adopt the merit system rather than the seniority system.
グローバルプレーヤーは年功序列制度よりも能率給（能力主義）を採用する傾向にある。

【face】

> But to **face** danger or risk, or to die for something which is not right is foolishness, not courage. （p.32，4行目）
> 危険に直面したときや正義以外のために死ぬのは愚かな行為であり、勇気ではない。

face は動詞で「直面する」という意味です。米国のCBSテレビネットワークの長寿番組にFace the Nationという政治番組があります。faceは「面子」という意味でもよく用いられます。面子という意味でのfaceは中国語から英語（イギリス）に入ってきたことばです。

One must face the facts of life.
人生に直面しなければならない（逃げてはならない）。

【remark（s）】

> He is ready to exchange witty **remarks** with the enemy.（p.34. 6行目）
> 敵と気のきいたやり取りをかわす余裕がある。

remark は「意見」や「言及」を意味しますが、opening remarksやclosing remarksなど特定の会の「開会や閉会のあいさつ」を指します。

Who should we ask to make opening remarks for the reception?
どなたにレセプションの開会のあいさつをお願いしたらいいでしょうか。

【supply】

> When Kenshin heard about Shingen's problem, he decided to **supply** him with salt, even though they were at war.（p.34. 17行目）
> 謙信はその話（信玄の）を聞き、戦いの最中だったにも関わらず塩を送った。

supply「供給する」は、supply A with B「AにBを提供する」という意味でよく使われます。provide A with Bも同様です。また名詞で supply and demand「需要と供給」という表現は頻繁に出てきます。suppliesと複数形で「生活必需品」を意味します。

My company deals with office supplies.
弊社は事務用品を取り扱っている。

【requirement】

> Many times both Confucius and Mencius said that the highest **requirement** of a ruler of men is to be kind and good.（p.38. 4行目）
> 支配者にもっとも必要とされるのは思いやりと善なる心だ。

requirementは「必要条件」のことです。

The construction company tries its best to meet customer requirements.
その建設会社は顧客の条件に合わせようとベストを尽くしている。

【warn】

> We were **warned** against being too kind without the right amount of correct judgment and justice.（p.42, 9行目）
> 適切な正しい判断と正義なしにただ優しすぎるだけなのは戒められた。

warnは「警告する」、「注意をする」ことを意味します。warningは「警告や戒めの忠告」を意味し、このwarningを複数回もらうと解雇につながります。

Don't tell me I didn't warn you.
だから言ったじゃないですか。

With one more warning, you'll be fired.
あと一度警告通知を受けたら、君はクビです。

米国にSurgeon General's Warningと言われるものがあります。「米国公衆衛生局が出す注意書き」です。たとえばタバコのパッケージにある "Cigarette causes lung cancer." がそれです。

【due to】

> It is said that **due to** the influence of music there was no cruelty in that part of the country.（p.48, 5行目）
> 音楽のおかげでその地方には残虐行為が起こらなかったという。

due toは「～の理由のために」という原因を表しています。他に owing toや内容的に「～のおかげで」という感謝の意味が入ってくると thanks toなども使われます。

Lunch appointment was cancelled due to a traffic accident.
交通事故でランチの予約はキャンセルになった。

Part II
Chapter 6 — Chapter 9

Chapter 6

Politeness

All foreign tourists have noticed that the Japanese people are very polite. Politeness is good if it shows sympathy for the feelings of other people. It should also show respect for social positions, which were originally due to actual merit, not birth. In its highest form politeness is close to love. Politeness is patient, kind, does not envy, does not praise itself, is not proud, behaves correctly and does not allow evil. One must know, however, the difference between true and false politeness.

When correct behavior became essential, it was natural that a system of etiquette should become popular. It was used to train young people how to bow, walk, sit and serve tea. Table manners became a science. Serving and drinking tea came to be a ceremony. A man of education was expected to master all of these things.

■merit 名利点　■envy 動ねたむ　■praise 動 ～をほめる　■essential 形最も重要な　■bow 動おじぎする

第6章

礼

　外国人の観光客は皆、日本人が大変礼儀正しいことに気がつく。真の礼には、他者の感情に対する共感が表れる。また、社会的地位に対する尊敬の念として表れることもあるが、それは、社会的地位がそもそも生まれではなく、実際の価値に基づくものだったからである。礼は、最高の形で表れる時、限りなく愛に近づく。礼は寛容にして慈愛あり、礼は妬まず、礼は誇らず、驕らず、非礼を行わず、己の利を求めず、憤らず、人の悪を思わず。一方、真の礼と偽りの礼の違いを知っておくこともまた必要である。

　正しい立ち居振る舞いが不可欠になれば、礼法（礼儀作法）がもてはやされるのはごく自然なことである。かつては、礼法に従い、お辞儀や歩き方、座り方やお茶の点て方について若者を訓練したものだった。食事のテーブルマナーは学問に、お茶を点て、いただくことは礼式になった。教育を受けた者は、これらすべてをマスターすることが求められた。

Some Europeans, however, have spoken badly about our etiquette. They say that we think about it too much and follow it too strictly. There may be some unnecessary points about ceremony. But is it any more foolish than strictly following the ever-changing fashions of the West? I think even fashions are not foolish. They simply show that human beings are always looking for something beautiful. Even more so, I do not think that ceremony is completely unimportant. It expresses the best way of achieving something, a result of long practice. The best way is the most economical and the most graceful. One man defined grace as the most economical manner of motion. The tea ceremony shows the best way to hold a bowl, a spoon, a napkin and so on. It may look boring or tiring but we soon realize that it's the best way to save time and labor. It is therefore the most graceful.

Etiquette and ceremony are outward signs of inner spiritual discipline. I will not touch on the origins and motives of our ceremonies. But I would like to emphasize the moral training which is involved. Etiquette became very detailed, so much so that various groups had their own special way of doing things. But the essential points were all the same. The best known group, the Ogasawara, said that the purpose of all etiquette is to train the mind. So even when you are sitting quietly, not even a violent person can upset you. This means that, by constant exercise in correct manners, one brings

■strictly 副 厳しく、きっちりと ■define 動 ～を定義する ■outward 形 外側の
■discipline 名 鍛錬 ■motive 名 動機、真意 ■so much so that 非常にそうなので
〜

けれども、ヨーロッパには、私たちの礼法について悪く言う人もいる。私たちがあまりにもそのことを気にしすぎ、きっちり従おうとしすぎると言うのだ。礼式に関しては、不必要な点もいくつかあるかもしれない。だが、絶え間なく変わる西洋のファッションを追い続けることより馬鹿げていると言えるだろうか？　私はファッションでさえ、馬鹿げているとは思わない。ファッションは、人間は常に美しいものを探し求めるということを示しているにすぎないからだ。ましてや、私は礼式がまったく無意味であるなどとは思わない。礼式は、何事かを成し遂げようとする時の最も良い方法、つまり、長期にわたる稽古の結果を表しているのだ。最も良い方法は、最も無駄がなく、最も優雅だ。あるひとは、優雅さとは最も無駄のない動きである、と定義している。茶道は、茶碗や茶杓、袱紗＊といった品々を持つための最も良い方法を示している。退屈で骨が折れるように見えるかもしれないが、すぐに、時間と手間を省く最も良い方法であることがわかるだろう。だからこそ、最も優雅なのである。

　礼法と礼式は、内面の精神修養が表に現れたものだ。私は私たちの礼式の起源や目的について触れるつもりはない。だが、礼式に関わる精神的な訓練については強調しておきたい。礼法は大変細かくなり、いくつもの流派が、それぞれ自分たちのやり方で行うようになった。けれども、本質はまったく変わらない。最も知られた流派である小笠原流によれば、あらゆる礼法の目的は、精神修養だという。だから、もし、静かに座っている時に暴力的な者に遭遇したとしても、心が乱されることはない。このことは、正しい立ち居振る舞いを絶えず稽古するこ

＊袱紗（ふくさ）　物を包んだり覆ったりする方形の布。慶弔時に持参する熨斗袋（のしぶくろ）などを包む。

mind and body together into perfect order and harmony with one's environment. The spirit should always be the master of the flesh.

If what we said, that gracefulness is economy of motion, is true, then constant practice of it must bring with it a reserve of motion. Fine manners, therefore, means stored power at rest. A good example is *Cha-no-yu*, the tea ceremony. Sipping tea is a fine art. It began with the mystical thinking of a Hindu hermit. It brings about calmness of mind, a clear and peaceful mood, and quiet behavior. These are the first essentials of *Cha-no-yu* and, without doubt, the first conditions of right thinking and right feeling. The small room in which it is done is itself a great help to direct one's thoughts away from the world. It is clean, simple and cut off from the sights and sounds of the noisy world. The simple interior does not distract one's attention like the various and many things in a Western room. The *kakemono* calls our attention more to grace of design than to beauty of color. The tea ceremony was created by the hermit during a time of war and was more than just a pastime. Before entering the quiet room, the soldiers taking part in it laid aside their swords together with thoughts of battle and cares of government. In the little room they found peace and friendship.

■reserve 图 蓄え、保留　■sip 動 すする　■mystical 形 神秘的な　■hermit 图 隠遁者　■distract 動（人）の気を散らす　■pastime 图 気晴らし　■take part in 〜に参加する　■lay aside 脇に置く

とで、精神と肉体の両方が完璧な状態になり、環境と調和するようになることを意味している。精神は常に肉体の主でなければならない。

　もし、優雅さが無駄のない動きであるということが正しいとすれば、絶えず稽古することで、動きは抑制されるようになる。洗練された身のこなしとは、つまり、力を静かに蓄えておくということに他ならない。その良い例が茶の湯——茶道である。茶をいただくことは芸術である。それはヒンドゥー*の隠遁者の瞑想を発端とし、心の平安と明晰かつ穏やかな気分、そして静かな物腰をもたらす。これこそが茶の湯の最も重要な点であり、間違いなく、正しい思考と正しい感情に最も適した状態なのである。茶の湯が行われる小さな部屋そのものが、世間から気持ちをそらす役目を担っている。部屋は清潔で、簡素で、騒々しい世間の景色や音から切り離されている。簡素なインテリアは、種々雑多なものが置かれた西洋の部屋とは違い、私たちの注意を妨げはしない。掛け物が我々の視線を惹きつけるのはそのデザインの優雅さであって、色彩の美しさではない。茶道は戦国時代に隠遁者によって創られたが、単なる娯楽以上の意味を持っていた。客として招かれた武士は、静かな部屋に入る前に、刀と共に、戦場についての考え事や、政（まつりごと）に関わる心配事も脇に置いていった。小さな部屋のなかに、武士は平和と友情を見出したのであった。

*ヒンドゥー教　バラモン教の流れをくむ多神教。インドやネパールでは多数派。

Cha-no-yu is more than a ceremony—it is a fine art, poetry in motion. Most importantly, it is a discipline for the soul of man.

Politeness gives grace to manners. But its function does not stop there. Suitable behavior comes from goodness and is put into action by tender feelings toward other people—a graceful expression of sympathy. It says that we should cry with those who cry and be happy with those who are happy. It is seen in the fine details of everyday life, sometimes unnoticed. For example, if you are out in the hot sun with no shade over you and a friend passes by, you stop him to say hello. He was carrying an umbrella but while he talks with you he is not holding it over his head. So now he is also in the sun, unprotected, like you. One might say, "How foolish!" but that's not the point. By his action, he is saying to you that he sympathizes with you. He would take you under his umbrella if it were big enough but it's not so he decides to share your discomfort. Even a small act like this shows thoughtful feeling.

■function 名機能 ■suitable 形適切な ■unnoticed 形気付かれない ■shade 名日陰 ■pass by 通り掛かる ■discomfort 名不快感

茶の湯は礼式以上の意味を持っている——それは芸術であり、動く詩である。何より一番重要なのは、人間の魂の鍛錬であるということだ。

　礼は、身のこなしに優雅さを与えるだけでなく、それ以上の機能を有していた。ふさわしい態度は高潔さから生まれ、他者への思いやりの気持ちが実際の行動に移させる——つまり、心遣いが優雅に表されているのだ。泣いている人がいれば共に泣き、喜んでいる人がいれば、共に喜ぶ。それは日常の些細なことのなかに見られ、しばしば見過ごされてしまう。たとえば、あなたが、暑い日に、覆いのないところにいたとする。そこに友人が通りかかる。あなたは彼に声をかけ、彼は立ち止る。彼は日傘を持っているが、あなたと話している間、さそうとはしない。だから、今や、彼もあなたと同じように、覆いがない状態で太陽の下にいる。「なんて馬鹿なことを！」と言うひとがいるかもしれない。でも、話の要点はそこではない。彼は自分の行動を通して、あなたに同情していることを伝えようとしているのだ。もし傘が充分大きければ、彼はあなたを傘に入れるだろう。だが、そうではないので、彼は不快な状況をあなたと分かち合うことにする。このような小さな行動のなかにも、思いやりの気持ちが表れている。

Another Japanese custom should be mentioned. It is often misunderstood by superficial writers on Japan. In America, when you present a gift to someone, you tell the other person how nice it is. In contrast, the Japanese way of thinking is that no gift is nice enough for the person receiving it. We want the other person to accept it not because it is good or nice but only as a small symbol of our feeling. The American speaks of the material of which the gift is made; the Japanese values the spirit in which it is given.

In the same way that a book cannot be judged by its cover, a standard of behavior should not be judged by the least important of its examples or types. Which is more important, to eat or to observe rules about eating properly? Which is more important, to tell the truth or to be polite? The Japanese are said to give an answer which is completely the opposite to what an American will say. But I must withhold comment until I discuss honesty and sincerity.

■superficial 形表面的な　■in contrast その一方　■properly 副適切に
■withhold 動差し控える　■sincerity 名誠意

もうひとつの日本人の習慣についても述べるべきだろう。それは、日本の上辺しか書こうとしない人々からしばしば誤解されてきたことである。アメリカでは、もし誰かにプレゼントを渡すとしたら、相手に対し、それがどんなにいいものなのかということを説明する。一方、日本人は、たとえどんなプレゼントであっても、プレゼントを受け取る人にふさわしいということはないと考える。私たちは、それがいいものだからではなく、ただ単に、自分の気持ちを表すささやかなものとして受け取ってほしいと願うのだ。アメリカ人はプレゼントの素材について話すが、日本人はプレゼントに込められた気持ちを大切にする。

　表紙で本の中身を判断できないのと同じように、行動規範について判断する時に、実例や形式を重視してはならない。食事をすることと、正しく食べるためのルールを順守することのどちらがより重要なのだろうか？　真実を言うことと、礼儀正しくあることのどちらがより重要なのだろうか？　日本人はアメリカ人とは正反対の答えを言うと言われる。だが、誠実と誠意について述べるまで、それについてのコメントは、控えさせていただくことにする。

Chapter 7

Honesty and Sincerity

Without honesty and sincerity, politeness is nothing. Doing the right thing beyond the proper bounds becomes a lie. If you are true to yourself, the gods will always watch over you. Sincerity is the beginning and the end of all things.

The *bushi* thought that his high social position was worthy of a higher standard of truth than ordinary people. *Bushi no ichi-gon* (the word of a samurai) could be trusted. His word alone was enough, without anything in writing. There are many thrilling stories about those who made the mistake of *ni-gon* (double talk) and paid for it by dying.

Sometimes a warrior would swear in the name of a god or upon his sword. But the regard for truth was so high that the best of samurai looked upon an oath as something beneath his honor. Truth is sometimes sacrificed for the sake of being polite. If someone dislikes

■proper bound 適切な範囲　■swear 動誓う　■oath 名誓い　■sacrifice 動 ～を犠牲にする　■for the sake of ～のために

第7章

誠

　誠実と誠意なくして、礼はない。一線を越えて正しいことを成した
としても、それは嘘になる。もし、あなたが自分自身に対して誠実で
あるならば、神々はいつもあなたを見守ってくださるだろう。誠実こ
そがすべての始まりであり、終わりである。

　武士はその高い社会的地位ゆえに、誠実に関し、一般の人々よりも
高度な規範に従う価値があると考えていた。武士の一言（武士の言葉）
には信用があった。言葉だけで充分であり、書面は一切不要であった。
二言（二枚舌）のミスを犯し、死をもって償うというスリリングな話が
いくつも残っている。

　武士は神の名や自分の刀に誓うこともあったが、誠実に対する畏敬
の念があまりにも大きかったため、一流の武士は、誓いの言葉を自分
の名誉に関わるものとして見ていた。ただし、誠実は礼の犠牲になる
こともある。もし誰かがあなたを嫌っているとして、あなたがその人

you and you ask him if he dislikes you, most people will tell a lie and say "I like you very much." But for the Japanese, this is different from *uso* (a lie). It was merely regarded as an empty form (*kyo-rei*).

I admit I am speaking now about the Bushido idea of truth. But we should also touch on the honesty of the business world, about which I have heard many complaints in foreign books and journals. It is true that loose business morals have given us a bad name but let us look at this carefully for future comfort.

Of all the great kinds of work in life, the one which was farthest from the warrior was that of the businessman. The businessman was of the lowest rank. Number one was the warrior, number two was the farmer, number three was the craftsman and number four was the businessman. The samurai could farm if he wanted to, but he hated any kind of business activity. We know the wisdom of this social arrangement because it prevented wealth from accumulating in the hands of the powerful. We also know that one cause of the fall of the Roman Empire was that people in power were also permitted to do business. This resulted in money and power being in the hands of a few families.

Business in feudal Japan, however, did not develop in that way. The disgrace attached to that kind of work attracted people who did not care much about social position. "Call a man a thief and he will steal." The commercial business people had a moral system

■admit 動 ～を認める　■complaint 名 不満、苦情　■comfort 名 心地よさ、慰め
■prevent 動 防ぐ　■accumulate 動 蓄積する

に自分を嫌っているか訊いたとする。ほとんどの人は嘘をついて「あなたのことが大好きです」と言うだろう。だが、日本人にとっては、これは嘘ではなく、単なる虚礼と見なされる。

　確かに、私は今、武士道における誠実ということについて述べているが、商業世界における誠実についても触れるべきだろう。これについては、海外の本や雑誌で批評されているのをよく目にする。商業道徳がルーズなせいで、私たちの評判が悪いことは事実であるが、将来のためにも、これについて考察してみたい。

　この世におけるさまざまな職業において、武士から最も遠かったのが商人だった。商人の地位は最下位だった。一番目が武士、二番目が農民、三番目が職人、そして、四番目が商人であった。武士は、本人が望む場合には農業をすることはあったが、商業活動については、いかなる種類のものであっても、忌み嫌った。この社会構造は、非常に優れたものであった。なぜなら、権力者が財力を持つことができないようになっていたからだ。ローマ帝国が崩壊した理由の一つは、権力者がビジネスを行うことを許されていたことにある。その結果、富と権力の両方が、少数の家族に委ねられることになったのだ。

　日本の封建時代におけるビジネスは、そのような形で発展したわけではなかった。その種の職業は不名誉なものだと考えられていたので、社会的な地位について関心のない者だけがビジネスに携わった。つまり、「人を泥棒と呼べば、彼は盗むであろう」という言葉通りであった

among themselves. With it they developed such things as the bank, insurance, etc. But in their relations with people outside of their business, they lived up to their bad reputation. So when the country was opened to trade, only the most adventurous and those with no idea of what is right and wrong rushed to the ports. Was Bushido not able to do anything about the dishonor of the business world? Let us see.

Those who know Japanese history will remember that only a few years after some of the ports were opened to trade, feudalism came to an end. The samurai's land was taken from them and in return they were given money. They were free to use that money for business. We would expect, then, that they would bring their values into business relations and reform the bad practices. Those who had eyes to see could not cry enough, those who had hearts to feel could not sympathize enough because many honest samurai failed in their business attempts. They failed because they lacked the skill to deceive, a skill which their rivals had mastered. We know that 80% of business attempts in America fail. So it is no wonder that only 1 in 100 samurai succeeded in business in Japan. Bushido values could not be applied to business and unbelievable amounts of money were lost. It was soon clear that the ways of wealth were not the ways of honor. But how were they different?

■insurance 名保険 ■live up to（期待などに）かなう ■reputation 名評判
■dishonor 名不名誉 ■reform 動改善する、改める ■bad practice 悪い習慣
■deceive 動欺く、だます

のだ。営利事業においては、関係者間の道徳体系は確立されており、それに合わせて銀行や保険といったものも発達していた。だが、事業関係者ではない者に対しては、悪い評判通りの行いをしていた。そのため、国が開国した時に港に集まったのは、よほどの冒険好きか、善悪の概念のない者だけであった。ビジネス世界の名誉を欠く行いに関して、武士道で規範することはできなかったのか。さてどうであろう。

　日本の歴史を知る人であれば、いくつかの港が開港した後、ほんの数年で封建制度が終わったことを覚えているだろう。武士の領地は没収され、代わりに金が与えられた。彼らは自由にその金を商売に使うことができた。それならば、彼らの価値観を商売関係に持ち込み、過去の悪習慣を正したに違いない、と思うかもしれない。だが、見ることができる目を持つ者はこれ以上泣けないほど泣き、感じることができる心を持つ者はこれ以上心を痛めることができないほど心を痛めたのだった。なぜなら、大勢の誠実な武士が商売に失敗したからである。彼らが失敗したのは、だます能力――彼らのライバルがマスターしている能力――に欠けていたためであった。アメリカでは80％の商売の試みは失敗に終わる。であるならば、日本でビジネスに成功した武士が、百人中たった一人であったのも頷ける。武士道の価値観をビジネスに持ちこむことは適わず、信じられないほど多くの金が失われることになった。富を得る方法は名誉を得る方法とは異なるということが、すぐに明らかになったのだった。だが、いったいどのように異なるのだろうか？

In Bushido there was no economic honesty because business was not a part of it. There was no political honesty because it could hardly develop under a feudal system. In Bushido there was only philosophical honesty and this was the highest kind of honesty. With all my sincere regard for the business honesty of the Anglo-Saxon race, I am told the reason is that "honesty is the best policy." It **pays** to be honest. So isn't this virtue its own reward? If it is followed because it brings in more cash than dishonesty, I'm afraid Bushido would rather tell lies!

Truth owes its growth largely to the world of business. Honesty is the youngest of the virtues and is the child of modern industry. Honesty proved to be a profitable virtue to practice. In the early days of trade, German goods were unreliable in regard to both quality and quantity. But now we hear very little of German carelessness and dishonesty in trade. They finally learned that honesty pays and our businessmen also have found out the same thing.

Often I have wondered if the truth of Bushido had any motive higher than courage. Lying was not a sin but was called a weakness and, as such, highly dishonorable. Honesty is intimately related to honor. So I think I should pause for a few moments to consider this aspect of Knighthood.

■sincere 形 誠実な、偽りのない、 ■reward 名 褒美 ■dishonesty 名 不正直、不誠実 ■unreliable 形 信頼できない、頼りない ■dishonorable 形 不名誉な ■intimately 副 親密に

武士道においては、経済的な誠実というものは存在しなかった。ビジネスとは無関係だったからである。政治的な誠実というものも存在しなかった。封建制度の下では発展する余地がなかったからである。武士道においては、哲学的な誠実しか存在していなかったが、これこそが、誠実のなかで最高のものだと考えられていた。アングロサクソン系の人々に、彼らにとっての商業的な誠実の根拠を尋ねるとこう言われる——「正直は最善の策」。正直であるほうが儲かるというのだ。徳はそれ自体が報いなのではないのか？　もし、正直であるほうが不正直であるよりもより多くの現金をもたらすという理由で追随されているのであれば、武士道は嘘をつくほうを選ぶだろう！

　誠実は主に、ビジネスの世界で成長を遂げた。誠実は、徳のなかでも最も歴史が浅く、近代産業の申し子である。誠実は実際に利益をもたらす徳として認められている。貿易の初期のころにはドイツ製の商品はその質、量共に信頼できないものであったが、今ではドイツ製の製品に不注意、あるいは不誠実な点はほとんど見られなくなった。彼らは遂に、正直であることは儲かるのだということを学んだのだ。そして、日本のビジネスマンたちも同じことを発見したのだった。

　しばしば思うのだが、武士道において誠実は勇気よりも高い動機があるのだろうか。嘘をつくことは罪ではないが、弱さと考えられており、非常に恥ずべきことと見なされていた。誠実は名誉と密接な関係にある。そこで、しばらくの間、武士道における名誉について考えてみたいと思う。

Chapter 8

Honor

A sense of honor had to be very much a part of the samurai character. They were educated to value the duties and privileges of the warrior class. The idea was taught to them by such words as *na* (name; upholding one's name), *men-moku* (face—not to lose face through shame), and *gai-bun* (outside hearing—hearing about a person's respectability in public). Anything which damaged one's good name was felt as shame. This sense of shame (*ren-chi-shin*) was one of the earliest things to be learned. "You will be laughed at," "It will disgrace you," "Are you not ashamed?" were the words used to correct bad behavior. The child felt these words strongly, as though he had learned them in his mother's womb. This sense of shame seems to me to be the earliest sign of moral awareness of a race. It is also closely connected with strong family feeling. The worst thing that the human race experienced very long ago was the awakening

■uphold 動持ち上げる、掲げる　■lose face 面目を失う　■in public 人前で
■womb 名子宮

第8章

名誉

　名誉の感覚は武士の人格形成において、非常に大きな部分を担っていた。彼らは、武士階級の務めと特権を重んじるよう教育された。その思想は、名（名を上げること）、面目（恥によって面目を失わないようにすること）、外聞（世間での評判について聞こえてくること）といった言葉によって教えられた。いかなることであれ、名を汚すことは恥であると考えられた。この恥の感覚（廉恥心）こそ、最も早い段階で教わるものだった。「笑いものになるぞ」「面目を失うぞ」「恥と思わないのか？」といった言葉が、誤まった行いを正す時に用いられた。子供はまるで、母親の子宮にいる時から知っていたかのように、こうした言葉を強く胸に刻んだのだった。この恥の感覚は、人類に道徳意識が芽生えた最も初期の段階からあったであろうと私は考えている。それはまた、家族に対する強い感情と密接に結びついている。ずっと昔に人類が体験した最悪のことは、恥の感覚の目覚めであった。私たちが初めて感じた恥の感覚はいちじくの葉に象徴されている。それでもっ

of the sense of shame. Our first sense of shame is represented by the fig leaf. With it we felt we must cover the nude body. A samurai who had experienced a slight humiliation when he was young did not let it change his character. He felt that if it were not corrected, it might lead to worse things. The early shame made him a better person because he did not let it continue.

In every samurai the fear of disgrace was very strong, even to the point of being cruel, which was not part of Bushido. At the slightest or imagined insult, a short-tempered man would use his sword to kill. There is a story of a well-meaning ordinary person who told a samurai that there was a flea on his back. There really was a flea but since fleas are usually found on animals, the samurai was insulted and killed the other person. The story may have been invented just to scare people. In any case, it shows the strong sense of shame which had developed in the warriors. Such a story is an extreme case, not the norm.

■fig leaf イチジクの葉、覆い隠すためのもの　■humiliation 图辱められること、屈辱　■insult 图侮辱　■well-meaning 形善意の　■flea 图ノミ　■in any case とにかく

て、裸の体を隠さなければならないと感じたのだ。武士に関して言え
ば、幼い頃に少しばかり辱められたからといって、そのせいで人格が
変わるようなことはなかった。正されずにいたなら、より悪い結果に
なると考えられていたからだ。幼い頃の恥は武士をより良い人間にし
た。なぜなら、二度と同じ間違いをしなかったからだ。

　どの武士も、侮辱を受けることに対し、強い恐怖心を抱いていた。武
士道では認められていない冷酷非道な行いも辞さないほど、その感情
は強いものだった。ほんの僅かでも侮辱されたと感じただけで、短気
な者は刀を抜いて、相手を切り殺した。こんな話がある。一人のあり
ふれた善良な人が、武士に向かって背中に蚤がいるぞ、と言った。実
際に蚤はいたのだが、蚤は通常であれば動物にしか見つからないもの
なので、武士は侮辱されたと感じ、相手を殺してしまった。この話は、
単に人を怖がらせるための作り話かもしれないが、いずれにしても、武
士が持っていた強い恥の感覚をよく表している。このような話はもち
ろん極端な例であって、一般的なものではない。

This kind of cruel excess in regard to honor was strongly counterbalanced by generosity and patience. It was considered to be very bad behavior to get angry because of something small and unimportant. There was a popular saying, "To bear what you think you cannot bear is really to bear." The great Ieyasu gave us some good things to think about: "The life of a man is like going a long distance with a heavy load upon the shoulders. Do not be in a hurry. Do not point out the faults of others. Be forever watchful of your own faults. To be patient and endure the difficulties of the world is the secret of long life." And he was a good example of what he said. Mencius taught us that anger because of something small is unworthy of a superior man. But anger for the sake of a great cause is just.

Other people have given us great things to think about: "When someone speaks badly about you, do not do the same in return; rather think about what you have done wrong." Or "When others blame you, do not blame them also; when they are angry at you, do not return the anger; joy comes to you only when strong feelings leave you." Still another is "Heaven loves all men equally; you should love others in the same way that you love yourself; make Heaven your partner and do your best." Some of these sound like Christian thoughts. They show us that natural religion is close to revealed religion. These were not only sayings but the very fiber of action.

■excess 名行き過ぎた行為　■counterbalance 動釣り合いを取る　■generosity 名寛容さ　■heavy load 重い荷物　■point out 〜を指摘する　■endure 動耐える　■fiber 名本質

この種の名誉に関わる過剰な冷酷さは、寛容さや忍耐などとうまく
バランスが取れている。小さな、重要でないことのために怒ることはと
てもよくないことだと考えられていた。有名な格言に「ならぬ堪忍する
が堪忍」というのがある。偉大な家康公は意味深い遺訓を残している。
「人の一生は重荷を負うて遠き道を行くがごとし。急ぐべからず。己を
責めて人を責むるな。堪忍は無事長久の基」。彼は自ら説いた通りの人
生を送った。孟子は次のように言っている。「小事に怒るは君子の愧ず
るところにて、大義のための憤怒は義憤である」

　他にも名言はたくさんある。「人の誣うるに逆らわず、己が信ならざ
るを思え」。あるいは、「人は咎むるとも咎めじ、人は怒るとも怒らじ、
怒りと慾とを棄ててこそ常に心は楽しめ」。まだもう一つある。「天は
人も我も同一に愛したもう故、我を愛する心をもって人を愛するなり。
天を相手にして己を尽くせ」。この言葉は、まるでキリスト教の言葉の
ように聞こえる。自然宗教が啓示宗教にいかに近いかということをよ
く表している。こうした言葉は単なる格言に留まらず、まさに行動の
本質を表しているのだ。

Very few people achieved this height of generosity, patience and forgiveness. Also, only a few men realized that honor exists within each person. It was easy to forget one's honor in the heat of action. Each man should love honor but should also remember that it is not something outside of oneself. Much of that which men call honor is not good honor. Too often the goal toward which young men strived was fame or pride in oneself. Many young men left home and vowed not to return until they had become famous and many ambitious mothers told their sons the same thing. The youngsters therefore would go through any kind of mental or physical suffering in order to achieve their goal. They wanted honor early—at a young age. One young son of Ieyasu was placed not at the front but at the rear of the army when an attack was made on a castle. When the castle fell, he cried bitterly because he was not at the front to win honor and fame. One man told him he would have other chances in the future but he angrily replied that he would never be 14 years old again! For this, a boy would give up his life.

■height 名高さ　■in the heat of ～の最中に　■strive 動励む、邁進する　■in oneself それ自体で　■vow 動誓う　■ambitious 形野心のある　■bitterly 副激しく、ひどく

ごく少数の者だけが、寛容、忍耐、赦しのこのような高みにまで到達できる。また、ごく少数の者だけが、誰もが名誉を内に秘めていることを理解している。興奮している時には、名誉について忘れがちである。誰もが名誉を愛することが望ましいが、名誉が自分の外に存在するものではないことを忘れてはならない。世間で言われる名誉の多くはよくないものである。多くの場合、若者が努力して目指すのは、名声か、自分のプライドを満たすものである。大勢の若者が家を離れ、故郷に錦を飾るまで、家には戻らないと誓う。また、大勢の野心的な母親が息子に向かって同様のことを言う。そのため、若者は目標を達成しようと心身共に苦痛を味わうことになる。彼らは早く、つまり、若いうちに名誉を得ようとする。家康の若い息子は、城が攻撃された時、軍の前方ではなく後方に回された。城が落ちると、軍の前方に配置されず、名誉と名声を得ることができなかったと言って悔し涙を流した。ある者が、これからいくらでも機会があるではないかと言ったところ、なんと彼は怒ってこう答えた。「14歳には二度となれないではないか」。名誉と名声のためならば、彼は喜んで命を捨てたに違いない。

Chapter 9

The Duty of Loyalty

Feudal morals have similarities with other systems of ethics but loyalty is the most special. It is the respect and duty given to one's lord. Being faithful is a virtue which exists among all kinds of people. But it is only in chivalry that it reaches its highest importance.

Hegel thought that loyalty should be shown to people (a nation), not to one person. Bismarck thought it was a German virtue but also one of other countries. In America our feeling for loyalty cannot be appreciated because all people are thought to be equal. In the same way that justice in one country may be considered injustice in another country, loyalty as we think of it may not be admired elsewhere. This is not because our idea is wrong but because it is, I'm afraid, forgotten. It is also because we carry it to a degree not reached in any other country. In China, to obey one's parents was the first duty. In Japan the first duty was loyalty to one's lord.

■ethics 名 道徳律　■faithful 形 誠実な、真心を尽くす　■admire 動 〜を称賛する
■elsewhere 副 他の場所で　■degree 名 度合い、レベル

第9章

忠義

　封建制度における道徳が、他の倫理体系と似かよっている点が多い
なかで、忠誠心は最も独特なものである。それは、主君への敬意と務
めを意味している。誠実であるということは、すべての人に共通した
徳ではあるが、武士道において、最も重要視されたのであった。

　ヘーゲル*は、忠誠心とは国民（国家）に対して持つものであり、一個
人に対してではないと考えた。ビスマルクは、ドイツだけでなく、他
の国々にとっても徳であると考えた。アメリカでは、忠誠心が評価さ
れることはない。なぜなら、すべての人民は平等であると考えられて
いるからだ。ある国では正義であっても、別の国では不正と見なされ
るかもしれないのと同じように、私たちが思うところの忠誠心も、他
の場所では称賛されないかもしれない。これは何も私たちの考えが間
違っているからではなく、忘れ去られてしまったためではないかと思
われる。また、私たちが忠誠心を、他のどんな国にも例を見ない高み
にまで引き上げてしまったせいかもしれない。中国では両親に従うこ
とが、第一の務めであるが、日本では主君への忠誠が第一の務めであ
る。

---

*ゲオルク・ヴィルヘルム・フリードリヒ・ヘーゲル（1770-1831）　ドイツの観念論哲学者。『精神現象学』『法
　哲学』などを著した。

There is a story which may shock my readers. It is about one of the greatest characters of our history, Sugawara Michizane. He was a victim of jealousy and false charges and was forced to leave the capital. His enemies also wanted to destroy his family. They began searching for his young son. They found out that he was being secretly kept at a school in a village. The master of the school was a man called Genzo, who was a former follower and supporter of Michizane. Genzo was ordered to deliver the head of Michizane's son on a certain day. But Genzo tried to find someone else instead. He looked carefully at all of the boys in the school but not one of them resembled Michizane's son. But at last he found another boy who looked like Michizane's son. On the appointed day an officer came to the school to identify and receive the head of the boy. This officer's father had also been in the service of Michizane and the two of them knew about the situation of Michizane's son. From the time when Michizane was forced to leave the capital, the officer was forced to be in the service of the enemy of Michizane. When he arrived at the school he identified the head as being that of Michizane's son, but in fact the head was that of his very own son. The officer himself could not be untrue to his new and cruel master but his own son could be the way to save Michizane's son. When the officer returned home that night he told his wife to be happy because their son had been of service to Michizane.

■victim 图 犠牲者　■jealousy 图 ねたみ、嫉妬　■deliver 動 職務を遂行する
■resemble 形 ～に似ている　■appointed 形 (日時などが) 指定された　■untrue 形
忠実でない

読者にショックを与えるかもしれない話を紹介したい。日本史に残る最も偉大な人物の一人、菅原道真についての話である。彼はねたみを買い、濡れ衣を着せられ、都を追われる。敵方は彼の家の断絶を計り、彼の幼い息子を探し始める。やがて、とある村の寺子屋に密かに匿われていることを突き止める。寺子屋の校長は名を源蔵といい、かつては道真の家来であった。源蔵は、指定された日に道真の息子の首を持ってくるよう命じられ、身代わりを探そうとする。寺子屋中の少年たちの顔を注意深く観察するが、誰一人として、道真の息子には似ていない。だが、遂に、似た者が見つかる。指定された日に、役人が首の確認と受け取りのため、学校を訪れる。この役人の父親も以前は道真の家来であったため、道真の息子の置かれた状況については二人ともよく分かっていた。道真が都を追われて以来、役人は道真の敵方に仕えるよう強制されていた。寺子屋に到着すると、役人は首が道真の息子のものであることを確認する。だが、実は、それは自分の息子の首だったのである。役人は、自分が新しい冷酷な主人に逆らうわけにはいかないが、自分の息子であれば、道真の息子を救う手立てになれると考えたのだ。その晩、帰宅すると、役人は妻に向かって、喜べ、息子が道真殿のお役に立てたぞ、と声をかけるのだった。

You may think this is a terrible story but the parents of the boy (and the boy himself) knew that he closely resembled Michizane's son. They had decided that the young boy should be a sacrifice so it was not just Genzo who had decided his fate. It was an example of total submission to loyalty to one's lord, much the same as Abraham's intended sacrifice of Isaac in the Bible.

Individual thinking in the West places importance on the separate interests of father and son, husband and wife and so on. But Bushido held that the interests of the family as one unit are the most important things. Even so, this natural feeling was below loyalty to one's lord. There are many stories about the deep emotional struggles between loyalty to one's family and loyalty to one's lord. Many people would rather die than make such a difficult decision. The Japanese *kō* (filial piety) is very strong. But in such conflicts of the heart, loyalty to one's lord was the higher virtue. Even mothers encouraged their sons to sacrifice everything for their lord.

Bushido took the position that society or the state was here before the individual. A person must live and die for it or for its leaders. The individual is the servant of the state. Bushido shares these ideas with such great men of the past as Aristotle and Socrates. The difference is that Bushido says that society is represented by a personal being and loyalty is the ethical result of this idea.

■sacrifice 名 犠牲　■submission 名 服従、従順　■interest 名 利害　■struggle 名 奮闘、葛藤　■filial 形 子としての、（親に対して）子の関係の　■piety 名 敬愛、孝心　■conflict 名 葛藤、対立

この話を酷い話だと思うかもしれないが、少年の両親(そして、少年自身)は少年が道真の息子にそっくりなことを知っていたため、彼を犠牲にすることを決めたのであって、源蔵一人が少年の運命を決定したわけではなかった。これは主君に対する絶対服従の一例であり、聖書に書かれたアブラハムがイサクを犠牲にしようとした話*と非常に似ている。

　西洋の個人主義の考えでは、父と子、夫と妻などの関係においては、個々人の利害に重きが置かれる。だが、武士道では、一単位としては、家の利害が最も重要だと考えられていた。にもかかわらず、この自然な感情でさえ、主君への忠誠心よりも下に位置づけられていたのである。家への忠誠と主君への忠誠の間で苦悩する話がたくさん残されている。あまりにも困難な決断を下す代わりに、死を選ぶ者が多かった。日本人の孝(子の親への忠義)の情は大変強いものであるが、そのような心の葛藤においては、主君への忠誠が優先された。母親でさえ、主君のためならすべてを犠牲にせよ、と息子を促した。

　武士道は個人に先立つものとして、社会や国が存在していた時代のものである。個人は国や社会、あるはその指導者のために生き、死ななければならなかった。個人は国の僕（しもべ）であった。このような武士道の理論はアリストテレスやソクラテスといった過去の偉人たちの理論に通ずる。両者の違いは、武士道では、社会は個人によって代表され、忠誠心はそのような考えの倫理的な結果であるとした点にあった。

---

*アブラハムがイサクを生け贄にしようとした話　旧約聖書『創世記』で、神がアブラハムの信仰を試すために、息子のイサクを生け贄にと命じ、アブラハムはそれに従った。神は直前で生け贄を救い、アブラハムを祝福した。

Even among so democratic a people as the English, the feeling of personal loyalty to a man and his descendants comes from the feeling their Germanic ancestors had for their chiefs. This has now passed more or less into their loyalty to royalty.

But in all of this let us not confuse loyalty to the lord who lives on the land and loyalty to the king who lives in our hearts. We can be faithful to both. Christians obey worldly rulers and their Lord at the same time. "Give to Caesar the things that are Caesar's and give to God the things that are God's." One must follow his country and his conscience. If the state ever grows so powerful as to take away our conscience, we are doomed!

Bushido did not require us to make our conscience the slave of any lord or king. Any man who allowed that to happen had a low social standing. He was hated as a *nei-shin* (unreliable supporter) or *chō-shin* (flattering "yes-man"). When a follower differed in opinion from his master, the loyal path for him to pursue was to use every available means to persuade him of his error. If he fails, the master may do with him as he wills. In cases of this kind, it was usual for the samurai to make the last appeal to his lord by showing his sincerity with his own blood.

One served his master with his life, which was based on honor. This is how the education and training of a samurai was conducted.

■descendant 名子孫　■worldly 形世俗的な　■doomed 形絶望的な　■slave 名奴隷　■social standing 社会的地位　■flattering 形お世辞の　■differ 動異なる

民主的だと考えられているイギリス人でさえ、個人およびその子孫に対する忠誠心を受け継いでいるが、これは、彼らのゲルマン民族の祖先が族長に対して抱いていた感情に由来するものだ。この忠誠心は、今日では、程度の差こそあれ、王室への忠誠という形で継承されている。

　だが、このことにおいて、地上に住む主君と、私たちの胸の内にある君主への忠誠心を混同しないようにしなければならない。私たちは両者に対して忠実でいることができる。クリスチャンはこの世のルールと同時に、彼らの神に従っている。「カエサルのものはカエサルに、神のものは神に」。誰もが自分の国と自分の良心に従わなければならない。もし、国の力があまりにも強大になり、私たちの良心が奪い去られるようなことになれば、万事休すである！

　武士道では、主君や君主のために良心を犠牲にすることは要求されなかった。そのようなことをする者は蔑まれ、佞臣（信用できない家臣）あるいは寵臣（こびへつらう“イエスマン”）として憎まれた。家臣が主君と意見を違えた場合には、誠意ある家臣であれば、何とか主君を説得しようとした。だが、もし説得に失敗すれば、主君は家臣を好きなように処分できた。このような場合に、家臣が自らの血をもって誠意を示すことにより、主君に最後の訴えをするのはごく普通のことであった。

　命を賭けて主君に仕えることは名誉なことだと考えられていた。この考えに基づき、武士の教育および訓練が行われた。

役立つ英語表現 2

【achieve】

It expresses the best way of **achieving** something, a result of long practice.（p.60, 8行目）
それ（礼式）は何事かを成し遂げようとする時の最も良い方法、つまり、長期にわたる稽古の結果を表しているのだ。

achieve は「達成する」という意味です。名詞は achievement です。

It is important to give employees a sense of achievement.
社員に達成感を与えることは重要である。

【attention】

The *kakemono* calls our **attention** more to grace of design than to beauty of color.（p.62, 14行目）
掛け物が我々の視線を惹きつけるのはそのデザインの優雅さであって、色彩の美しさではない。

attentionは「注意、注目」のことで、draw an attentionで「注意を喚起する」という意味。会議や集まりで騒がしいときに "May I have your attention, please?" と言って静かにしてもらうのは決まった使い方です。

I'd like to draw your attention to this figure in the chart.
表のこの数字に注目してください。（プレゼンのときなどに）

【mention】

> Another Japanese custom should be **mentioned**. （p.66, 1行目）
> もう一つの日本人の習慣についても述べるべきだろう。

mentionは「述べる、触れる」という意味です。

> As I mentioned earlier, please be sure to fill out the questionnaire before you leave.
> 先ほども申し上げましたが、お帰りになる前にアンケートに記入をお願いいたします。

【withhold】

> But I must **withhold** comment until I discuss honesty and sincerity.
> （p.66, 14行目）
> だが、誠実と誠意について述べるまで、それについてのコメントは、控えさせていただくことにする。

withholdは「差し控える」という意味です。また「源泉徴収する」という意味でも使われています。

> Income tax is automatically withheld from your payment .
> 所得税は自動的に給料から源泉徴収されます。

【for the sake of】

> Truth is sometimes sacrificed **for the sake of** being polite. （p.68, 13行目）
> ただし、誠実は礼の犠牲になることもある。

for the sake ofは「～のために、～の目的で」の意味です。

> For the sake of argument, let's tentatively say that smoking in public should be completely banned.
> 議論の便宜上、仮に、公衆の場では全て禁煙にするということで始めてみましょう。

【touch on (upon)】

> But we should also **touch on** the honesty of the business world.
> （p.70，4行目）
> 商業世界における誠実についても触れるべきだろう。

touch on は「〜の点に触れる」という意味でプレゼンなどの説明では頻繁に用いられます。

> Let's touch on (upon) the background of this project.
> このプロジェクトの背景について触れておきましょう。

【result in】

> This **resulted in** money and power being in the hands of a few families.
> （p.70，18行目）
> その結果、富と権力の両方が、少数の家族に委ねられることになったのだ。

result in 〜 は「〜の結果になる」という意味です。lead to 〜 も同様の意味で用いられます。

> His around-the-clock working resulted in a sales increase.
> 昼夜問わず一心不乱に働いた結果、売上が上昇した。

【live up to】

> But in their relations with people outside of their business, they **lived up to** their bad reputation. （p.72，2行目）
> だが、事業関係者でない者に対しては、悪い評判通りの行いをしていた。

live up to は「〜に応える」という意味です。

The new hire tried her best to live up to the manager's expectations and she was stressed out.
新入社員はマネージャーの期待に沿うようにベストを尽くしたのでストレスで参ってしまった。

【owe A to B】

> Truth **owes** its growth largely **to** the world of business. (p.74, 10行目)
> 誠実は主に、ビジネスの世界で成長を遂げた。

owe A to Bは「Aの内容はBのおかげである」という意味です。個人的にお金を借りたときや、立替てもらったときなどには

> How much do I owe you?
> おいくらですか。

といいます。ちなみにIOUはインフォーマルな借用書のことで I Owe You. からきたものです。

【awareness】

> This sense of shame seems to me to be the earliest sign moral **awareness** of a race. (p.76, 11行目)
> ずっと昔に人類が体験した最悪のことは、恥の感覚の目覚めであった。

awareness は「目覚めること、気がつくこと」を意味します。形容詞の aware「気づいている、承知している」は、説明のときによく使う表現です。

> As you may be aware, profits rose sharply in the second quarter.
> お気づきのように、第2四半期の利益は急増しました。

【patient】

> To be **patient** and endure the difficulties of the world is the secret of long life.（p.80, 9行目）
> 堪忍は無事長久の基。

patientは「我慢強い、忍耐強い」の意味ですが、名詞のpatienceは口頭でもメールやビジネスレターでも、「しばらくお待ちください」の意味でよく用いられます。空港のアナウンスでもよく聞く表現です。

> Thank you for your patience.
> しばらくお待ち下さい。

【go through】

> The youngsters therefore would **go through** any kind of mental or physical suffering in order to achieve their goal.（p.82, 9行目）
> そのため、若者は目標を達成しようと心身共に苦痛を味わうことになる。

go throughは「経験する、体験する」の意味で用いられます。

> The company had to go through many difficulties in order to be listed.
> その会社は困難を経て、上場されることになった。

go throughは「目を通す」という意味でも多く出てきます。

> Please go through this newspaper article quickly before the meeting.
> 会議の前にこの新聞記事にさっと目を通しておいてください。

【loyalty】

Feudal morals have similarities with other systems of ethics but **loyalty** is the most special.　(p.84, 1行目)
封建制度における道徳が、他の倫理体系と似通っている点が多いなかで、忠誠心は最も独特なものである。

loyalty は「忠誠心」という意味です。またある特定のブランドしか買わないときも I'm loyal to ABC. などと使えます。

There is less and less loyalty to the company among the employees.
その会社の社員の忠誠心はどんどん薄くなっていった。

【make a decision】

Many people would rather die than **make** such **a** difficult **decision**.
(p.88, 13行目)
あまりにも困難な決断を下す代わりに、死を選ぶ者が多かった。

make a decisionは「決定を下す」という意味で、decision-making procedureというと「意思決定方法」でよくMBAのテキストなどに取り上げられています。

The manager finally made a decision as to whether to cut 100 employees.
そのマネージャーはついに100人の社員を解雇するか否かについて決断を下した。

【conflict】

But in such **conflicts** of the heart, loyalty to one's lord was the higher virtue. (p.88, 14行目)
そのような心の葛藤においては、主君への忠誠が優先された。

conflictは精神的な葛藤から戦争における国家間の対立まで「不一致」という意味で用いられます。身近なところではスケジュールが合わないという表現があります。

If you find any schedule conflicts, please let me know immediately.
もしスケジュールが合わない場合は、すぐにお知らせください。

Part III
Chapter 10 – Chapter 13

Chapter 10

The Education and Training of a Samurai

The first thing to be developed was character; of less importance was being careful in one's activities, intelligence and logic. We touched on the value of such things as poetry, but these were accessories and not essentials of samurai training. A superior mind was highly regarded but the word *Chi* referred to wisdom more than knowledge. The three things which supported Bushido training were *Chi* (wisdom), *Jin* (goodness) and *Yū* (courage). A samurai was essentially a man of action. He was concerned with science only in regard to weapons. Religion was important only in giving him courage. Literature was mainly a pastime. Philosophy was of help in the formation of character or in regard to some military or political problem.

■logic 名論理　■accessory 名付属物　■be concerned with ～に関係している
■be of help 役に立つ

第10章

武士の教育および訓練

　最も重要視されていたのは人格の形成であり、思慮深い態度や知性、論理などには、あまり重きが置かれていなかった。詩などの価値については前に述べたが、武士の教育においてはあくまで付帯的なものであり、本質的なものではなかった。すぐれた知性は高く評価されたが、「智」という言葉は、知識というよりは知恵を意味していた。武士道は智（知恵）、仁（思いやり）、そして勇（勇気）の三つによって支えられていた。武士は基本的には行動する人間でなければならなかったため、学問は武器に関することに限られていた。宗教は勇気を与えてくれる点だけが重要であった。文学は主に娯楽であった。哲学は、人格の形成や軍事、あるいは政治における問題が起きた時に役立てられた。

Studies consisted of learning how to use the sword, the bow and arrow, the spear; how to ride a horse; military tactics, jūjutsu, calligraphy, ethics, literature and history. Of these, jūjutsu and calligraphy were particularly important—calligraphy for its artistic value and as an indication of a person's character; jūjutsu as knowledge of one's body for the purpose of self-defense.

■consist of ～から成る　■spear 名槍　■tactics 名戦術、戦法　■calligraphy 名書道　■indication 名表れ

教育科目は刀、弓矢、そして槍の使い方、馬術、兵法、柔術、書道、
倫理、文学、そして歴史であった。なかでも柔術と書道は——書道は
その芸術的価値と人格の表現手段として、柔術は護身を目的とした人
体に関する知識として——重要だと考えられていた。

Chapter 11

Self-Control

We were taught not to show any emotion due to sorrow or pain. We should be polite to others by not expressing our own troubles. This became a part of our national character but this should not be misunderstood. It may be true of some people some of the time but I do not think it can ever be true of a whole nation. In this regard, to the foreign observer, we may seem hard-hearted but we are really as capable of tender emotion as any race under the sky.

In one way I think we have to feel more than others because to hold back emotion is suffering itself. Imagine children brought up in that way—does it make them stronger or more sensitive? One description of a great character is that the person shows no sign of joy or anger. Even the most natural feelings were kept under control—a father wanting to embrace his son, a husband wanting to kiss his wife. At least what one did in front of others was different

■sorrow 名悲しみ、悲哀　■in this regard この点で　■hard-hearted 形薄情な
■hold back（事実・本心などを）隠す　■description 名描写、表現　■embrace 動
～を抱き締める

第11章

自制心

　私たちは、悲しみや苦痛といった感情を表に出してはならないと教わってきた。相手のことを気遣って、自分の苦しみは隠しておくべきだ、と。これが、日本人の国民的な性格の一部となった。だが、誤解してはならない。ときにはそれが当てはまる人々もいるだろうが、国民全体にあてはまるとは言い切れないだろう。それに、日本人のそういった点は、外国人の目から見れば、薄情者と映るかもしれない。しかし、私たち日本人は、この空の下のどんな民族にも負けないほど、人を思いやる心を持っている。

　ある意味において日本人は、他の民族よりも感じることが多いはずだ。というのも、感情を隠すことが、苦痛そのものだからである。そんな風に育てられた子供たちを想像してみよう。子供たちはたくましく育つだろうか、それとも繊細に育つだろうか。「喜怒色にあらわれず（喜びや怒りが顔にあらわれない）」、というのが偉人を描写するときの言いまわしだった。父親が息子を抱きしめたいと思う気持ちや、夫が

from what he did in private. There may be truth in what someone said—American husbands kiss their wives in public and beat them in private; Japanese husbands beat theirs in public and kiss them in private!

Calm behavior and a calm mind should not be disturbed by passion of any kind. I remember when, during the recent war with China, a large group of soldiers left one town. Many people went to the station to see them off. An American also went there, expecting to see loud demonstrations. The whole nation was highly excited and there were fathers, mothers, wives, and sweethearts in the crowd. But nothing happened. The people only bowed deeply in silence. You could hear a few people crying only if you listened very carefully.

In everyday life also, I know of a father who spent whole nights listening to the breathing of a sick child. He stood behind a door so that he might not be caught in such an act of parental weakness. There was also a mother who, in her last moments of life, did not send for her son so that he would not be disturbed in his studies.

■disturbed 動邪魔をする、気をそらす　■of any kind いかなる種類の　■see someone off （人）を見送る　■sweetheart 名恋人　■parental 形親の

妻にキスをしたいと思う気持ちといった、もっとも自然な感情ですら抑えつけられた。すくなくとも家のなかですることと、公衆の面前ですることは区別された。誰かが言ったが、「アメリカ人の夫は人前では妻とキスし、家のなかでは妻を殴る。日本人の夫は人前では妻を殴り、家のなかではキスする」というのはあながち嘘ではないだろう。

　冷静な振る舞いや冷静な心は、どんな情熱にもかき乱されてはならない。先の中国との戦争（日清戦争）＊で、ある連隊が街を出発したときのことを思い出す。彼らを見送るために大勢の人々が駅にやってきた。ひとりのアメリカ人もやってきたが、彼は、駅に別れの挨拶が響きわたるのを期待していた。日本中が戦争に沸き立っていたし、見送りの人々のなかには兵士たちの父母や妻や恋人がいたからだ。しかし、期待はずれだった。人々は黙って深々と頭を下げるだけだった。そっと耳を澄ましてみれば、何人かのすすり泣きが聞こえたかもしれない。

　日々の生活においても、病気の子供の息づかいに耳を傾けながら何日も夜を徹した父親がいる。親の弱さをあらわす振る舞いを気づかれないよう、襖のかげに隠れて立っていたという。いまわの際にあっても、勉学の邪魔になってはいけないと息子を呼び寄せようとしなかった母親もいる。

＊**日清戦争**（1894–1895）　朝鮮半島の支配権をめぐる日本と清国との戦争。日本が勝利し、下関条約が締結され講和が成立。日本は遼東半島および台湾・澎湖諸島と、賠償金2億両を得た。

Even when a man or woman feels something deeply moving in his or her soul, it is quietly controlled and is not expressed in speech. It is truly harsh to Japanese ears to hear sacred words expressing secret heart experiences. One young samurai wrote in his diary that if you have such feelings, you should not disturb them with speech. Let them work alone quietly and secretly. If we put those feelings into words, it is taken by us as a sign that they are not deep or sincere. As one Frenchman said, speech is often the art of concealing thought.

If you call on a friend in time of deepest trouble or suffering, he will always receive you laughing with red eyes or wet cheeks. If you ask him what is wrong, he may say something like "They who meet must part" or "He who is born must die." But he will not say such things unless you press him. To laugh is an effort to regain balance at an unlucky time, as if to oppose the misfortune with an equally strong force.

■harsh 形耳障りな ■sacred 形神聖な ■conceal 動隠す ■call on （人）を訪問する ■as if あたかも～かのように ■misfortune 名逆境

男女にかかわらず、心の底から感動したときでさえ、胸のなかにおさめて言葉には表さないようにする。心のなかのひそやかな出来事を語るのは神聖なことばであるべきで、それを軽々しく聞くのは日本人にとって耳障り以外のなにものでもなかった。「心のなかに感情が芽生えたら、その感情を言葉で妨げてはいけない」と、ある若い侍が日記に書いている。静かに、ひそかに、感情が働くままにしておくのだ、という。日本人にとって、感じたことを言葉にするのは、深くもなく誠実でもないことのしるしと受けとられた。あるフランス人が言ったように、しゃべることは「思いを隠す技術」なのである。

　深い悲しみや困難のさなかにある友人を訪ねれば、その友人は目を赤くし、頬を涙でぬらしながらも、いつもと変わらない笑みを浮かべて迎えてくれるだろう。何かあったのかと尋ねれば、友人は、「会者定離（会うものは必ず離れる運命にある）」とか、「生者必滅（生命あるものは必ず死滅する）」といったようなことをつぶやくかもしれない。だが無理やり問いたださないかぎり、そんなことすら口にしないだろう。笑いは、逆境にあって心のバランスをとろうとする努力のあらわれであり、不幸を同じだけの強い力で押し返そうとしているようなものだ。

One way of expressing our emotions, however, is through poetry. A mother who tries to comfort her broken heart imagines her dead child to have gone on a dragonfly chase. She sings softly to herself "I wonder how far he has gone today, my little hunter of the dragon-fly?" I will not mention any more examples because it is difficult to express in a foreign language the feelings that have come from the bleeding human heart, drop by drop.

I hope I have to some extent shown the inner working of our minds. It often appears to be hard or a mixture of laughter and sadness, and its soundness is sometimes questioned. It has been suggested that our endurance of pain and lack of worry about death are due to having less sensitive nerves. If that is so, why? One can imagine various reasons but personally I think it is because we were originally very excitable and sensitive and we recognized the need to control ourselves.

Training in self-control, however, can easily go too far. It can have a bad effect on the soul and can make a beautiful character ugly. The ideal we should observe is to keep the mind level. The highest point of self-control is best illustrated in the first of the two things we shall discuss in the next chapter.

■dragonfly 名 トンボ　■bleeding 形 出血する　■drop by drop 一滴ずつ
■excitable 形 興奮しやすい　■go too far 度を超す　■ugly 動 醜くする、見苦しくする　■illustrated 動 説明する、解説する

ともあれ、私たちの感情をあらわすすべもあり、そのひとつが詩歌である。ある母親（加賀千代女）は、死んだわが子はトンボを捕りに出かけていったのだと想像して、傷ついた心を慰めようと句を詠んだ。「蜻蛉つり今日はどこまで行ったやら」。他の例をあげるのはやめておこう。なぜなら、一滴一滴血をしたたらせるように胸から絞りだされた思いを、外国語に翻訳するのは難しいからだ。

　日本人の心の働きを、ある程度は紹介できただろうか。それは一見冷酷であったり、笑いや悲しみが入り混じっているように見えたりして、ときには正気を疑われることもある。日本人が苦痛に耐え、死に対して無頓着なのは、鈍感だからではないかという人もいる。もしもそれが真実ならば、なぜ日本人は鈍感なのだろう。いろんな説があるだろうが、私個人の考えでは、日本人はもともと激しやすいうえに繊細な心を持っているので、感情を抑えなければならないことを自覚したからではないかと思う。

　しかし、自制心の訓練は度を越してしまいがちだ。そんな場合は、精神に悪い影響を与えたり、立派な性格をゆがめたりしてしまう可能性がある。守るべき理想は、心の平安を保つことだ。次の章では二つの制度をとりあげるが、そのうち最初の制度に、自制心の極致がよく現れている。

Chapter 12

Suicide and Revenge

The form of suicide discussed here is *hara-kiri* and correcting wrong things is *kataki-uchi* in Japanese. Many foreign writers have written about these. To cut open one's stomach may sound terrible to foreign ears. But it also exists in literature outside of Japan so it should not be so strange. In our minds this way of dying is associated with the noblest of actions and the most touching sadness. We therefore do not think that it is terrible.

The choice of the stomach was based on an old belief that it was the center of the soul and the feelings. When Moses, David, Isaiah, Jeremiah and other inspired men of old spoke of the bowels, they all supported the belief of the Japanese that the stomach was the holy place of the soul. The Semites always spoke of the liver and kidneys and the surrounding fat as the place of emotion and of life.

■suicide 图自殺（すること）■revenge 图復讐、敵討ち ■be associated with 〜と関係がある ■touching 形人の心に触れる ■inspired 形飛び抜けて素晴らしい ■Semite 图セム人 ■liver 图肝臓 ■kidney 图腎臓

第12章

切腹と敵討ち

　ここで取り上げるのは、自殺の形式である「ハラキリ（切腹）」と、過ちを正す方法である「敵討ち」だ。これまでに多くの外国人作家が、これらについて書き綴ってきた。腹を切り裂くと聞けば外国人はおぞましく感じるだろう。だが切腹は日本以外の国の文学にも存在するので、そんなに奇異なものではない。日本人の心のなかで、この死に方はもっとも気高い行為や胸をゆさぶられる悲しみと結びついている。そのために、切腹をおぞましいとは思わない。

　切る場所に腹を選んだのは、古くからそこに魂と感情が宿ると信じられているからだった。モーゼ*、ダビデ*、イザヤ*、エレミヤ*、その他聖書に登場する人物が腸について語っているが、それらはどれも「腹に魂が宿る」という日本人の信念を裏付けている。セム族は、肝臓や腎臓、そして周囲の脂肪を、感情と生命の宿る場所だと考えた。

*モーゼ　旧約聖書『出エジプト記』などに登場する、紀元前13世紀頃のイスラエル民族指導者。奴隷として使役されていたイスラエル人を率いてエジプトを脱出し、シナイ山で神から十戒を授かったとされる。「ヨセフその弟のために腸焚くるがごとく」は、モーゼが書いたとされる旧約聖書『創世記』の一文。

*ダビデ　古代イスラエル2代目の王(在位：前1000頃–前960頃)。イスラエルを統一し、首都をエルサレムに定めた。

*イザヤ　紀元前8世紀のイスラエルの預言者。旧約聖書『イザヤ書』の1〜39章までを書いたとされている。「腸が『鳴動する』」は、その『イザヤ書』の「それゆえ、わがはらわたはモアブのために（略）堅琴のように嘆く」(16-11)を指す。

*エレミヤ　紀元前7世紀から紀元前6世紀に活動したイスラエルの預言者。旧約聖書『エレミヤ書』を書いたとされている。「腸が『いたむ』」は、その『エレミヤ書』の「彼のゆえに、胸は高鳴り／わたしは彼を憐れまずにはいられないと／主は言われる」

The word *hara* meant not just stomach but to the Japanese and the Greeks alike the spirit of man was thought to live somewhere in that region. The people of old were not the only ones who thought in this way. It is not just superstition. It is more scientific than the general idea of making the heart the center of the feelings. Modern doctors speak of abdominal and pelvic centers of sensation. They refer to sympathetic nerve centers in those parts of the human body which are strongly affected by any spiritual or mental action. From this point of view, the idea of *hara-kiri* is "I will open the place of my soul and show you how it is. See for yourself whether it is dirty or clean."

I am not saying that suicide is right. But the high value placed on honor was the excuse for many who took their own lives. One foreign writer said that when honor is lost, it is a relief to die. So you can see that this way of thinking was not only in Japan. Death in regard to honor was accepted in Bushido as the solution for many problems. Even a natural death was seen as nothing at all and nothing to be wished for. I think that many good Christians, if they are honest, are fascinated by or admire the suicide of some people in their own history. Isn't it true that even the death of Socrates was partly suicidal? He believed the state was wrong. But even so he willingly obeyed the order to die, in spite of the possibilities of escape. He was not forced.

■region 图地域、地方 ■superstition 图迷信 ■abdominal 形腹部の ■pelvic 形骨盤の ■affected 形影響された ■relief 图安心（感）、安堵 ■fascinate 動〜を魅惑する ■in spite of 〜にもかかわらず

「ハラ」という言葉は、単に腹を指しているのではない。日本人やギリシア人にとって、そこは人間の精神が宿る場所だった。古代の人々だけがそんな風に考えたわけではない。単なる迷信でもない。ふつうは心臓に感情が宿ると考えるが、それよりはもっと科学的な考えである。近代の医者たちは、腹や腰のあたりに感覚の中心があると言う。それは人間の腹や腰に集まっている交感神経のことで、心の動きに強く影響される。この考え方でいけば、切腹というのは、「私の魂の宿る場所を開いて、どうなっているかごらんいただこう。汚れているか、それともきれいであるか、見て判断するがいい」ということになる。

　私は、自殺が正しいと言う気はない。しかし、名誉に重きを置く考え方は、多くの人が自ら命を絶つ理由になった。ある外国人作家は言った。名誉が失われたときは死ぬことが救いになる、と。つまり、日本人だけがこのような考え方をするわけではないのだ。武士道では、名誉にかかわる死は多くの問題を解決すると信じられている。自然な死には何の意味もなく、そんな死に方は誰も望まなかった。多くの善良なキリスト教徒も、正直なところ、歴史上の人物の自決に心を惹かれ、敬意を感じているのではないかと思う。
ソクラテスの死も半ば自殺だったのではないだろうか。彼は国の命令が間違っていると信じていた。しかし、それでも——逃れる可能性だってあったのに、進んで死刑という命令に従い、自ら毒杯をあおった。

Now I think my readers will understand that *hara-kiri* was not only a suicidal process. It was a legal ceremony. It started in the middle ages. It was a way by which warriors could pay for their crimes, apologize for mistakes, get their friends back, or prove their sincerity. When they were legally forced to do it, it was done with ceremony. This form of self-destruction could be done only by those who were totally calm about it. It was therefore suitable for the *bushi*.

I thought I might give a description of the ceremony. But it has already been done by a much better writer than I, so I will use his words (Mitsford, in his *Tales of Old Japan*). He watched one of the ceremonies himself.

"We (7 foreign representatives) were invited into the main hall of the temple where the ceremony was to be performed. In front of the high altar a red rug was laid on the floor. The light from the candles was dim but enough to see. Seven Japanese took their places on the left and we on the right. No other person was present. After a few minutes, Taki Zenzaburo, a strong-looking young man 32 years of age, walked into the hall wearing his ceremonial dress. He was accompanied by a *kaishaku* and three officers who also wore their special dress. The *kaishaku* was a pupil of Taki Zenzaburo. They both bowed to the 14 of us; we bowed in return. Slowly and with great dignity the young man

■legal 形合法的な　■self-destruction 名自殺　■altar 名祭壇　■rug 名じゅうたん、敷物　■dim 形薄暗い　■take one's place 席に着く　■be accompanied by 〜に付き添われる　■dignity 名威厳、尊厳

さて、すでに読者のみなさんには、切腹が単なる自殺の方法ではなかったことをおわかりいただけただろう。切腹は合法的な制度だった。始まりは中世である。それは、武士が罪をつぐない、過ちを詫び、友を取り戻し、自分の誠実さを証明する行為だった。法律上の罰として切腹を命じられたときは、儀式が執り行われた。作法をもって自ら命を絶つやり方は、その場に際して決して取り乱したりしない人間にしか成し遂げることはできない。だからこそ、切腹は武士にふさわしいものとされた。

この儀式について、私自身の言葉で説明してみたいとも思う。だが、私よりもはるかに筆の立つ著者がすでに描写しているので、ここでは彼の言葉を借りたいと思う（『旧日本の物語』より。ミッツフォード著）。作者は切腹の儀式に立ち会った。

　　　われわれ（七人の外国人代表者）は、儀式が行われる寺院の本堂へ案内された。高い仏壇の前には赤い敷物が敷かれていた。ろうそくの灯りは薄暗かったが、儀式を見るには十分な明るさだった。七人の日本人検使が左の座に、われわれは右の座に着いた。他には誰もいなかった。しばらくして、見るからにたくましい、32才の滝善三郎*が礼装で本堂に入ってきた。一人の介錯人と、特別な礼装を着た三人の役人が付き添っていた。介錯人は滝善三郎の門弟である。二人は、日本人検使と外国人代表者の十四人に一礼し、われわれも礼を返した。ゆっくりと威厳にみちた動作で、善三郎は仏壇を背にして赤い敷物の上に正座した。介錯人はその左側に控えていた。役人のひとりが脇差と呼ばれる短刀を運んできた。善

---

*滝善三郎（1837-1868）　備前岡山藩士。1868年2月4日、同藩家老日置帯刀率いる藩兵約400人が西宮へ警護に向かう途中、フランス人水兵二人がその前を横切ろうとしたため、藩兵とフランス兵が衝突。神戸沖にいた列国軍と撃ち合いになり、外交問題にまで発展した（神戸事件）。砲術隊長であった滝は、その責任者として、切腹を命じられた。

seated himself on the red carpet with his back to the high altar. The *kaishaku* was on his left. One of the officers brought forward the *wakizashi*, the short sword. The young man received it, raised it to his head with both hands and placed it in front of himself. Then he spoke, with no emotion showing on his face. 'I, and I alone, gave the order to fire on the foreigners at Kobe, and again as they tried to escape. For this crime I now take my life. I beg all of you to honor me by watching the act.' Following this he allowed his dress to slip down so that he was naked from the waist up. He put his sleeves under his knees so that he would not fall backward (a noble man should die falling forward). He then took the sword and looked at it almost lovingly. He stabbed himself deep below the waist on the left-hand side. He pulled it across to the right side, turned it in the wound, and then gave a slight cut upwards. During these movements he never moved a muscle on his face. When he took the sword out, he leaned forward and stretched out his neck. For the first time an expression of pain crossed his face but he made no sound. At that moment the *kaishaku*, who was still at his side, jumped to his feet, raised his sword in the air, and with one blow the head was cut from the body. Dead silence followed, broken only by the sound of blood pouring out of the body. It was horrible! The *kaishaku* bowed. We were requested to confirm that the death sentence had been carried out. The ceremony was over and we left the temple."

■fall backward あお向けに倒れる　■lovingly 副 愛情を込めて　■stab 動 突き刺す ■dead silence 全くの静寂　■confirm 動 確認する　■death sentence 死刑　■carry out 実行［遂行］する

三郎はそれを受け取り、両手で恭しく頭の高さに押し頂いてから、自分の前に置いた。それから、何の表情も見せずに、口を開いた。「拙者は、神戸において外国人に発砲する命令を独断で出し、彼らが逃げようとするところを再び発砲させた。この罪の責任をとり、切腹いたす。ご検分、宜しくお願い申しあげる」。続いて、彼は着物を帯のところまで脱ぎ、上半身をさらけだした。両袖を膝の下に敷きこむのは、後ろに倒れないためだった（誇り高い武士が死ぬときは前に倒れるべきだと考えられていた）。善三郎はおもむろに短刀を手にとり、愛しげといってもいいような眼差しで見つめた。そして左の腹を深く刺し、そのまま右の腹に向かって切ると、いったん元に戻して上のほうへ少しだけ切り上げた。一連の動作の間、彼の顔はぴくりとも動かなかった。善三郎は短刀を引き抜き、前かがみになって首を伸ばした。はじめてその顔に苦痛の表情がよぎったが、声をあげることはなかった。その瞬間、それまでじっと控えていた介錯がやおら立ち上がり、空に刀をふりあげ、一撃のもとに首をはねた。場はしんと静まりかえり、ただ胴体から吹き出る血の音が響くばかりだった。なんと恐ろしい！介錯がお辞儀をした。われわれは、儀式が滞りなく行われたのを確認するよう求められた。儀式は終わり、われわれは寺院を後にした。

I could provide many more cases from literature or from people who saw them happen. But I think one more will be enough. Two brothers, Sakon (24) and Naiki (17) tried to kill Ieyasu for their father's sake. But before they could enter the camp they were taken prisoners. Ieyasu admired the courage of the youths and ordered that they should be allowed to die an honorable death. Their little brother, Hachimaro, only 8 years old, also had to die because the order applied to all male members of the family. All three were taken to the place where it was to happen. A doctor who was present at the time wrote this in his diary:

"When they were all seated, Sakon turned to the youngest and told him to go first so that he could make sure he did it right. But the little one replied that he had never seen it done so he would like to see his brothers do it so that he could follow them. 'Well said,' Sakon told him. 'You can be proud to be a child of our father.' Sakon and Naiki then both stabbed themselves in turn, each teaching the youngest what to do and what not to do. When both of the elder brothers had died Hachimaro calmly made himself naked to the waist and followed their examples."

■be taken prisoners 捕らえられる ■honorable 形名誉ある ■make sure 確認する ■Well said. その通りだ。 ■in turn 順に

文学作品や実際の目撃者の話から、さらに切腹の例を挙げることはできる。しかし、もう一例だけとりあげれば十分だろう。左近（24歳）と内記（17歳）という兄弟が、父の仇をとるために、徳川家康を殺そうとした。が、陣屋に忍びこもうとして捕えられた。家康は、若者たちの勇気を称え、名誉ある死を遂げさせよ、と命じた。二人の幼い弟、八麿はまだ八歳だったが、処刑は一族の男子すべてにおよぶものだったため、彼もまた切腹しなければならなかった。三人は、処刑場に連行された。その場に居合わせた医師が日記に書いている。

　　三人が座に着いたとき、左近は幼い弟に向かって「お前が最初にやりなさい。きちんと成し遂げたことを見届けてやるから」と言った。だが、弟は「私は切腹を見たことがありません。兄さんたちのお手本を見て、そのとおりにしようと思います」と答えた。「よく言った。お前はわれらが父の子であることを誇りに思え」と左近が言った。それから、左近と内記は順に自分の腹を刺し、「こうやるのだ」「こうしてはならぬ」と、末の弟に切腹の仕方を教えた。二人の息が絶えると、八麿はしずかに着物を腰まで脱ぎ、教えられたとおりに腹を切った。

Sadly, however, many hot-headed young men thought that this was a glorious way to die. Many took their lives for no good cause or reason. Life was thought to be cheap according to the popular standard of honor. But for a true samurai, to hasten or to invite death was the same as a man who lacks courage in facing danger, pain or difficulty. For a typical fighter, when he lost battle after battle and was chased here and there, when he found himself hungry and alone in the dark hollow of a tree, when his sword would no longer cut well, when his bow was broken and he had no arrows left, when all of these things came upon him, to die was to be weak and afraid. At such times he would cheer himself on with "Sorrows and pains, keep coming! Heap more and more upon my back! I do not want to miss even one test of the strength that remains within me."

This, then, was the Bushido teaching—Bear and face all bad luck and hardship with patience and a pure conscience. Mencius taught that when Heaven is about to place great trust in someone, it first exercises his mind with suffering and his muscles and bones with hard work; it makes him hungry and very poor; it curses his activities. True honor means to face and accept what Heaven gives, not to run away! Sir Thomas Browne wrote the exact English equivalent of what Bushido teaches: "It is brave to think of death as nothing but when life is more terrible than death, it takes even more courage to continue to live."

(⌒)

■hot-headed 形 性急な、短気な ■glorious 形 名誉となる ■hasten 動 急いで～する ■hollow 名 空洞 ■heap 動 ～を積み上げる ■hardship 名 困難、苦難 ■curse 動 ～をののしる ■equivalent 名 同等のもの

一方、残念なことに、切腹で死ぬのは名誉なことだと短絡的に考える若者が多かった。なんでもない出来事や理由で次々に若者が死んでいった。世間一般の名誉という基準で測っても、命は安物だった。だが真の武士にとって、死に急いだり死を呼び込んだりするのは、危険や苦痛や困難に立ち向かおうとしない臆病な行為と同じだった。ある典型的な武士は、次々と戦に敗れ、逃げる先々で敵に追われたとき、刀が欠けて切れなくなったとき、弓は折れ、矢も尽きたとき、気がつけばたったひとり暗い木のうろの中で飢えていたとき、また、これらすべてのことが身に降りかかったときでも、死ぬのは意気地なしだと考えた。そしてそんなときには「悲しみや苦しみよ、どんどんやってくるがいい！わが身に降り積もるがいい！この体に残っている力をことごとく試してやる」と、自らを励ました。

　そう、これが武士道の教えだ。忍耐と純粋な良心で、あらゆる災難や困難に立ち向かい、耐えること。それは孟子も教えていた。「天が重要な役目を人に与えようとするとき、まずその心を苦しめ、筋骨に重労働を与え、飢えさせ、貧しくさせ、行おうとすることに罵声を浴びせる」。真の名誉は、天が与える試練を逃げずに受け止めることだ！サー・トマス・ブラウン*は、武士道の教えとまったく同じような言葉を書いている。「死をなんでもないことと思うのは勇敢だが、生が死よりも恐ろしいときは、生き続けるほうに勇気がいる」

*トマス・ブラウン（1605-1682）　イギリスの医学者、哲学者。

It was important for a Japanese to take revenge on anyone who wronged his parents or his master. In revenge there is something which satisfies one's sense of justice. The person who takes revenge thinks that his good father should not have been put to death. He who killed him did great evil. "My father, if he were alive, would not permit such a thing to go unpunished. Heaven itself hates wrong doing. It is the will of my father and the will of Heaven that the evil-doer must die by my hand. Because he took my father's life, I, who am his flesh and blood, must take the life of the murderer." An eye for an eye; a tooth for a tooth. Until we carry it out, we feel a great sense of something left undone.

In Judaism there is a jealous God. In Greek mythology there is a goddess of revenge. But in Bushido people take action in cases which are not judged by ordinary law. The master of the 47 *rōnin* was sentenced to death and had no higher authority to appeal to. His faithful followers took revenge and they also were judged as wrong by the law. But popular feeling passed a different judgment and they are remembered even until this day.

Lao-tse taught us to return injury with kindness. But Confucius said that injury must be set right—revenge (but only for the sake of our superiors). One's own wrong-doings, including those to wife and children, were to be endured and forgiven.

■take revenge 復讐をする　■wrong 勔（人）を不当に扱う　■be put to death 処刑される　■go unpunished 罰を免れる　■will 图意志　■evil-doer 图悪事を働く人　■sentence to death 死刑判決を下す　■popular feeling 大衆感情

日本人にとって、自分の両親や主君を不当に扱った人間に復讐する
のは重要なことだった。復讐には人の正義感を満足させる何かがある。
復讐する者はこう考える。善良な父親が殺されるいわれはない。父親を
殺したやつは大罪を犯したのだ。「もし父上が生きていたら、このよう
な行為に何の咎めもないことを許さないだろう。天も悪事を憎む。大
罪を犯した者を私の手で葬るのは、父上の意志であり、天の意志なの
だ。やつは父上の命を奪ったのだから、血肉を分けたこの私が、やつ
の命を奪わなくてはならないのだ」。これこそ「目には目を、歯には歯
を」である。そうしないかぎり、私たちは何かをやり残した感覚につき
まとわれる。

　ユダヤ教には妬む神がいる。ギリシア神話には復讐の女神が登場す
る。しかし、武士道においては、法で裁けない事件に人々が立ち上が
る。赤穂浪士として知られる四十七士の主君は切腹を命じられたが、控
訴する上級裁判所のようなものはなかった。忠実な家来たちは仇討ち
をはたし、彼らもまた、法によって誤った裁きを受けた。だが民衆の
感情は法とは違う判決を下し、四十七士は今日もわれわれの記憶のな
かに生き続けている。

　老子は、怨みには徳を返すべき、と説く。かたや孔子は、怨みには
正義を返すべき――つまり復讐を説く。しかし、それは目上の者や恩
人のために行われる場合のみ、とされる。自分自身への不正な行為は、
妻子への不正な行為も含めて、耐え忍び、許さなければならなかった。

Both suicide and revenge lost their reason for being when the Criminal Code was made. No more do we hear of romantic stories involving the adventures of a young girl seeking the murderer of her parent; no more fighting between families making a wrong right; tales of wandering knights like Miyamoto Musashi are things of the past. Now it is the police and the law and there is no need for *kataki-uchi*. We do hear of *hara-kiri* from time to time. Probably it will continue to some extent as long as the past is remembered. Some people have said that in cases of very painful suicide, the person is not normal, likes unpleasant things, or is crazy. But the usual case of *hara-kiri* requires complete calmness and is not done by such people. Another person said suicide is either rational or irrational and *hara-kiri* is the former.

From these things, it is easy to conclude that the sword played an important role in social discipline and daily life and that it was, indeed, the soul of the samurai.

■criminal code 刑法 ■wamdering 形 さすらう ■from time to time 時々 ■as long as 〜する限り ■rational 形 理性的な、理にかなった ■irrational 形 非理性的な、理不尽な

切腹と敵討ちは、刑法が公布されたときに存在する理由を失った。若い娘が親の仇を探し続けるロマンチックな物語を耳にすることはもはやないし、仇同士の一族が義を正そうと争うこともない。宮本武蔵の武者修行も、今では昔話だ。現在それを肩代わりするのが警察と法で、敵討ちの必要はなくなったのである。切腹はときおり耳にする。こちらは過去の記憶が消えないかぎり、ある程度は続いてくのだろう。あまりにも苦痛を伴う自殺の場合、その人間は正常ではないか、そういうやり方を好んでいるか、あるいは錯乱状態だ、と言う人々もいる。だが正規の切腹にはこれ以上ない冷静さが必要で、そんな人間が行うことはありえない。別の意見では、自殺には理性的な自殺と非理性的な自殺があるというが、切腹は前者にあたる。

　これらのことから容易にわかるのは、刀が社会の規律や日常の生活に重要な役割をになっていたということだ。そして刀はまさに武士の魂であった。

Chapter 13

The Sword, the Soul of the Samurai

Bushido made the sword its symbol of power and bravery in battle. Very early the samurai boy learned to use it. For him it was a thrilling moment when, at the age of 5, he put on samurai dress and was given a real sword in place of the toy he had been playing with. From that time, whenever he went outside of his father's gates, he would wear it or a wooden one covered with gold as a symbol of his status. After a few years he always wore the real sword but not a sharp one. Soon after that he was given the real, sharp swords. He would happily go out to try their blade edges on wood and stone. When he became a man at the age of 15, his actions were free from control and he carried swords sharp enough for any work. Just having the swords gave him the feeling and appearance of self-respect and responsibility. What he carried in his belt was a symbol of what he carried in his mind and heart—loyalty and honor. The long sword

■put on（衣服を）身に着ける ■in place of ～の代わりに ■status 图地位、立場
■appearance 图出現 ■self-respect 图自尊心

第13章

刀、武士の魂

　武士道は、刀を力と武勇のしるしとした。武士の子供は幼いときから刀の使い方を学んだ。五歳になって武士の服装を身につけ、これまで遊んでいたおもちゃの刀の代わりに本物の刀をもらうのは、子供にとって胸おどる瞬間だった。そのときから、家の門をくぐって外に出るときは、武士の身分をあらわす刀、あるいはめっきの木刀をつねに腰に差していた。数年もすると本物の刀しか差さなくなるが、刃は研いでいない。その後まもなく、鋭い刃の刀を与えられる。少年は喜びいさんで外に出て、木や岩に向かって切れ味をためそうとするだろう。十五歳で成人になり、自由な行動を許され、どんな用にも耐えられるような鋭い刀を持ち歩くようになる。刀を持っているだけで、自尊心と責任感を覚え、それが態度にもあらわれた。彼が腰に差しているものは、心に抱くもの——忠義と名誉の象徴であった。長剣（「大刀」ある

(*daitō* or *katana*) and the short one (*shōtō* or *wakizashi*) were always with him. When at home they were within easy reach in any room and at night they were next to his pillow. They were his constant companions and were given names as objects of love. Any insult to the sword was an insult to the owner.

The maker of swords was an inspired artist and his shop was a holy place. Every day he began his work with prayer and purification. He put his soul and spirit into the forming of the steel. Every movement was a religious act. The sword thrills us (the surface, color, edge, curve of its back) in different ways. We feel its power and beauty. We also feel admiration and fear. Unfortunately, however, its use was too often improper, such as trying it on some harmless animal's neck.

■within easy reach すぐ手の届く所に　■prayer 图祈り、祈とう　■purification 图浄化　■admiration 图称賛　■improper 不適切な、間違った　■harmless 形無害の、罪のない

いは「刀」と呼ばれる）と短剣（「小刀」あるいは「脇差」と呼ばれる）は常に身の回りにあった。家にいるときは、手の届くところにあり、夜には枕元にあった。刀は忠実な友であり、愛情の対象として名前がつけられた。刀にたいする侮辱は持ち主にたいする侮辱であった。

　刀鍛冶は霊感を受けた芸術家であり、仕事場は聖域だった。毎日、身を清め神仏に祈りを捧げてから、仕事を始めた。魂と精神をこめて鋼鉄の刀を打った。どの瞬間も宗教的な行為だった。刀の、その鋼のおもて、色合い、刃先、刀身の反り具合といったものに、私たちはぞくぞくする。そこに力と美を感じるのだ。畏敬と恐れも。しかし、残念ながら刀は濫用されることが多かった。試し切りとして、罪のない動物の首に刃が振り下ろされることもあった。

But Bushido always stressed only its proper use. The wise man knew when it should be used, which was not often. Count Katsu was a good example. Many people tried to kill him. But he never made his sword dirty with blood. He once told a friend that he had a great dislike for killing people, so much so that he had not killed even one man. "There have been many," he said, "who should have had their heads cut off. But I let them all go. On purpose I made it difficult to draw my sword. Even though others would cut me, I would not cut back. Those other people are like fleas and mosquitoes. They bite, but what does that amount to? It itches a little but you won't die." These are the words of a person whose Bushido training took place during one of the bloodiest times of our history. His thinking was that the best won victory is when blood does not flow. He and others of similar mind show that, after all, the best ideal of knighthood was peace.

■on purpose 故意に　■mosquito 名蚊　■amount to 結局～になる　■itch 動～をイライラさせる　■after all 結局のところ

だが武士道がつねに主張するのは、刀の正当な使用だけだ。賢明な人は、どんなときに刀を抜くべきかを知っているし、その機会はめったにない。勝海舟伯*が良い例である。彼は何度も暗殺されかかった。しかし自分の刀を血で汚すことはしなかった。人を殺すのが嫌いも嫌い、大嫌いなのでひとりも殺したことがない、とかつて友人に語っている。「首を切り落とさなきゃならないようなやつは何人もいた。だがみんな放っておいた。細工をしてわざと刀を抜きにくくしておいた。相手が切りかかってきても、俺は切り返さなかった。そんなやつらはノミか蚊のようなもんだ。刺されたからってどれほどのものか。ちょっぴり痒いが、死にゃあしない」。これが、日本の歴史のなかでもっとも血なまぐさい時代だったころに武士道の教育を受けた人物の言葉である。「血を流さないで勝つことが最上の勝利」というのが彼の考え方だった。つまるところ、勝海舟伯や他の似たような考えの持ち主たちが教えているのは、武士道の究極の理想は平和であるということだ。

***勝海舟**（1823-1899）　江戸末期・明治の幕臣、政治家。1860年に咸臨丸を指揮して渡米。戊辰戦争では西郷隆盛と会見し、江戸無血開城を実現する。

役立つ英語表現 3

【for the purpose of】

> Of these, jūjutsu and calligraphy were particularly important—calligraphy for its artistic value and as an indication of a person's character; jūjutsu as knowledge of one's body **for the purpose of** self-defense. （p.102, 3行目）
>
> なかでも柔術と書道——書道はその芸術的価値と人格の表現手段として、柔術は護身を目的とした人体に関する知識として——重要だと考えられていた。

for the purpose ofは「〜のために」という意味です。

> For the purpose of implementing the market research, we need at least two more people.
> 市場調査を実行するために少なくとも、あと2名必要です。

【capable】

> In this regard, to the foreign observer, we may seem hard-hearted but we are really as **capable** of tender emotions as any race under the sky. （p.104, 5行目）
>
> それに日本人のそういった点は、外国人の目から見れば、薄情者と映るかもしれない。しかし、私たち日本人は、この空の下のどんな民族にも負けないほど、ひとを思いやる心を持っている。

capableは「能力のある、有能な」という形容詞で、人物評価では非常に高い評価を表す形容詞です。

> I'm lucky to have a capable assistant.
> 有能なアシスタント（秘書）がいて幸運である。

be capable of は「〜ができる」という可能を表します。

He's capable of speaking Arabic.
彼はアラブ語を話すことができる。

【under control】

> Even the most natural feelings were kept **under control**—a father wanting to embrace his son, a husband wanting to kiss his wife.（p.104, 12行目）
>
> 父親が息子を抱きしめたいと思う気持ちや、夫が妻にキスしたいと思う気持ちといった、もっとも自然な感情ですら抑えつけられた。

under controlは「支配下にある、管理下にある」という意味です。
反対はout of controlで「制御できない」という意味になります。

Everything is under control.
全て準備ができています。お任せください。

He is out of control.
彼は手がつけられない（手に余る）。

【in private】

> At least what one did in front of others was different from what he did **in private**.（p.104, 14行目）
>
> 少なくとも家のなかですること、公衆の面前ですることは区別された。

in privateは「内々に」という意味です。私的な状況で会うという意味ですが、通常は「他の人を入れずに2人だけでお話がしたい」という場面で使われます。

Can we talk in private?
ちょっと内々に2人でお話できませんか。

【disturb】

One young samurai wrote in his diary that if you have such feelings, you should not **disturb** them with speech. （p.108, 4行目）
「心の中に感情が芽生えたら、その感情を言葉で妨げてはいけない」と。

disturbは「妨げる、邪魔をする」などの意味で用いられます。

I'm disturbed by a false rumor about a private matter.
私的なことで間違ったうわさを流され煩わされている（嫌な思いをしている）。

次の文は、ホテルの客室のドアノブに必ず掛かっている札に書かれています。

Please don't disturb.
邪魔をしないでください（起こさないでください）。

【to some extent】

I hope I have **to some extent** shown the inner working of our minds.
（p.110, 8行目）
日本人の心の働きを、ある程度は紹介できただろうか。

to some extentは「ある程度」という意味です。同様の意味でto some degree とう言い方もあります。

The CEO touched upon the product's inadequacies to some extent but we felt he could have gone much further.
CEO（最高経営責任者）は欠点についてある程度、触れたが、私たちはもう少し踏み込んで話をしてほしかった。

【question】

> It often appears to be hard or a mixture of laughter and sadness, and its soundness is sometimes **questioned**. (p.110, 9行目)
> それは一見冷酷であったり、笑いや悲しみが入り混じっているように見えたりして、ときに正気を疑われることもある。

questionは動詞で「質問する」という意味が一般的ですが、「疑問に思う、疑わしい」という意味でもよく使われます。

> The newly hired engineer's qualifications were questioned by the committee after their discovery of a major oversight in the project.
> プロジェクトの中で、大きなミスが見つかったあとで、新任のエンジニアの資格に委員会は疑問を持った。

> newly hired=新任の　qualification=資格　oversight=ミス、見落とし

【have a bad effect on】

> It can **have a bad effect on** the soul and can make a beautiful character ugly. (p.110, 16行目)
> そんな場合は、精神に悪い影響を与えたり、立派な性格をゆがめたりしてしまう可能性がある。

have a bad effect onは「〜に悪影響を与える」という意味です。
effectは「結果、影響」のことで good effectは「よい結果、よい影響」となり、effectそのものに良い、悪いのイメージはありません。

> Just sitting at the desk working all day long certainly has a bad effect on one's health.
> 一日中、机に向かって仕事をするのは当然健康によくない。

【legal】

It was a **legal** ceremony. （p.116, 2行目）
それは（切腹は）合法的な制度だった。

legal は「合法的な、法律上の」という意味です。反対はillegal「違法の」です。

It's illegal to drive a car intoxicated.
酔っぱらい運転は違法だ。

【description】

I thought I might give a **description** of the ceremony.（p.116, 8行目）
この儀式について、私自身の言葉で説明してみたいと思う。

descriptionの動詞形describeは「描写する」という意味で覚えておくといいと
思います。日本語では「説明する」と訳すことが多いので、explainという単語と混
乱するときがあります。describeは「形や状況を説明する」、explain は「理由を
説明する」と覚えておきましょう。

Please describe what it looks like.
どういう様子か説明してください。

【carry out】

Until we **carry** it **out**, we feel a great sense of something left undone.
（p.124, 10行目）
そうしないかぎり、わたしたちは何かをやり残した感覚につきまとわれる。

carry outは「実行する」という意味です。implement a plan「計画を実行する」
という言い方も頻繁に出てきます。

Who can carry out such a big plan within a year?
誰がこのような大プロジェクトを1年以内に実行できますか？

【play a role】

From these things, it is easy to conclude that the sword **played an** important **role** in social discipline and daily life and that it was, indeed, the soul of the samurai. （p.126, 14行目）

これらのことから容易にわかるのは、刀が社会の規律や日常生活に重要な役割を任っていたということだ。そして刀はまさに武士の魂であった。

play a role は「～の役割を果たす」という意味です。play a role as mediator というと「仲介の労をとる」という意味です。

One of the foreign staff played an important role to promote the office morale.
外国人スタッフがオフィスの士気を盛り上げるのにひと役買った。

【in place of】

For him it was a thrilling moment when, at the age of 5, he put on samurai dress and was given a real sword **in place of** the toy he had been playing with. （p.128, 2行目）

五歳になって武士の服装を身につけ、これまで遊んでいたおもちゃの刀の代わりに本物の刀をもらうのは、子供にとって胸踊る瞬間だった。

in place of は「～の代わりに、代理で」いう意味です。同じ意味でforを使うことによって簡単に言うこともできます。

Due to an urgent matter, Mr. Yamada will travel to New York in place of me.
緊急の用事ができために、山田を代理として出席させます。

I'm calling for Mr. Yamada.
山田の代理で電話をかけています。

【take place】

These are the words of a person whose Bushido training **took place** during one of the bloodiest times of our history. （p.132, 11行目）

これが日本の歴史のなかでももっとも血なまぐさい時代だったころに武士道の教育を受けた人物の言葉である。

take placeは「行われる、起こる」という意味です。

The exhibition will take place in two months.
展示会は2ヵ月後に開催される。

【after all】

He and others of similar mind show that, **after all**, the best ideal of knighthood was peace. （p.132, 13行目）

つまるところ、彼（勝海舟伯）や 他の似たような考えの持ち主たちが教えているのは、武士道の究極の理想は平和であるということだ。

after allは「結局のところ」という意味ですが、いろいろ試した結果、やはりこうなってしまったというニュアンスがあります。

After all, it's your own problem.
結局はご自分の問題ですね。

Part IV
Chapter 14 — Chapter 17

Chapter 14

The Training and Position of Women

The way of thinking of a woman is sometimes said to be much different from that of a man. Men use reason; women do not. The Chinese character for "the mysterious" or "the unknowable" is written with two parts—one with "young," the other with "woman," because their delicate thoughts are beyond our ability to explain.

In the Bushido ideal of the woman, however, there is little mystery. On the one hand, she was like the Amazon women warriors of Greek mythology or legendary South America. She was tall, strong and ready to fight. On the other hand, she was thought to be suited for ordinary home life. She is represented by the Chinese character of a woman holding a broom. This was the main idea in Bushido (housework). The two ideas are quite different but they are not in disagreement with the rules of Knighthood, as we shall see.

■on the one hand 一方では　■legendary 名 伝説　■ready to 〜する心構えができている　■broom 名 ほうき　■in disagreement with 〜と相反して

第 14 章

女性の教育と地位

　女性のものの考え方は男性とはずいぶん違うと言われることがある。男性は道理を説くが、女性はそうではない。「神秘的」や「不可知の」という意味の漢字(「妙」)は、二つの部分から成り立っている。ひとつは「若い」という意味、もうひとつは「女性」だ。女性の繊細な思考は、男性の能力では説明できないからだ。

　しかし、武士道における女性の理想像には、神秘的なものはほとんどない。一方では、ギリシア神話か南米の伝説にでてくるような女戦士「アマゾネス*」のように、背が高くて、たくましくて、闘志満々である。だが他方では、家庭的だと考えられた。女性をあらわす漢字(「婦」)は箒という意味の字が含まれている。家事をする人というのが武士道の女性にたいする主な考え方だった。アマゾネス的であり家庭的であるというのは、かなり矛盾しているようだが、武士道においては対立しない。それをこれから説明しよう。

*アマゾネス　ギリシア神話に登場する女武者からなる部族。勇猛で好戦的。転じて、女傑の意にも用いる。

Bushido was a teaching mostly for men. The virtues it prized in women were far from being clearly feminine. Bushido praised most those women who could show heroic strength worthy of the strongest and the bravest of men. Young girls, therefore, were trained to control their feelings, to harden their nerves and to use weapons. They were especially taught to use the long-handled sword called *nagi-nata*. They had to be able to defend themselves if need be. The main purpose of this training was not for use in war. She was her own bodyguard. She protected herself as much as her husband looked after his lord. Her training was also of use in the education of her sons, as we shall see later.

The training with the sword and other similar exercises were healthy activities. But they had possible practical use as well. When girls became women they were given a knife. They might need to use it on an attacker or on themselves. If a virgin was attacked by someone, she did not wait for her father to come. She always carried her knife with her. It was a disgrace not to know how to kill herself to save her honor. She had to know the exact spot to cut in her throat. She had to know how to tie her legs together with a belt so that, if she were killed, she would be found in a proper position. Virginity was highly regarded as a virtue in the samurai woman. If she were taken prisoner in war and faced with being violated by the soldiers, she would pretend to agree. When she had the chance, she would run away and take her own life.

■if need be 必要とあれば　■as much as ～と同じ程度に　■virgin 图処女　■exact spot 正確な場所　■proper position 適切な姿勢　■violate 勔強姦する　■take one's own life 自らの命を絶つ

武士道は、もっぱら男性のための教えだった。女性に重んじられる
美徳も、女性らしさといわれるものとはほど遠かった。武士道が賞賛
したのは、もっともたくましくて勇敢な男性にふさわしいほどの勇ま
しさをもった女性であった。そのため、若い娘は感情を抑え、精神力
を鍛え、武器を手に取った。とくに「薙刀」と呼ばれる長刀の使い方を
習った。必要なときにはそれで自分の身を守ることができるようにな
らなくてはいけなかった。薙刀の稽古の目的は、戦場で使うためでは
ない。自分の身を守るためだ。夫が主君を守るように、妻は自分自身
を守った。それに子供の教育のためでもあった。それは後で説明しよ
う。

　剣術の稽古などは、健康によい運動でもあった。もちろん実際に刀
を使うこともある。少女が成人すると、短刀を与えられた。襲われる
ようなことがあれば、それで敵を刺したり、場合によっては、自分の
胸を刺したりした。貞操の危機ともなれば、父親がかけつけてくるの
を待ったりはしない。常に短刀を懐に忍ばせていた。名誉を守るため
の自害の方法を知らないのは恥であった。咽喉のどこを短刀で突き刺
すかを正確に知っておかなければならなかった。きちんと膝を閉じた
状態で亡骸が見つかるように、帯で両足を結ぶことを知っておかなけ
ればならなかった。武家の女性において、純潔は大事な美徳であった。
戦で敵方に捕らえられ、乱暴されそうになれば、その女性はおとなし
く従うふりをするだろう。そして隙を見て逃げ、自害するのだ。

A man's ideals were not the only ones thought suitable for a woman. Far from it! The gentle things of life were also required of them. Music, dancing and literature were not neglected. Some of the finest lines in our literature were written by women. Dancing (for samurai girls, not geisha) was taught to make their movements graceful. Music was for the delight of their tired fathers and husbands. It was not for the sake of the art itself. The even higher purpose of music was for purity of heart. The sound had to be in harmony with the player's heart. Here we see the same idea as that in the training of young people—moral worth was more important than the skill. Music and dancing were valued as bringing grace and brightness to life. They were not for building pride in one's ability.

The skills of our women were not for show or for climbing the social ladder. They were for entertainment at home—family or guests. Home life guided their education. They lived and worked hard for the honor of the home. As a daughter she sacrificed herself for her father, as a wife for her husband and as a mother for her son. So from earliest youth she was taught to deny herself. Her life was not one of independence but of dependent service. It sometimes happens that a young man falls in love with a young lady who returns his love with equal feeling. But when she realizes that his interest in her makes him forget his duties, she makes herself less attractive. Her purpose is that he will be less interested and pay more attention

■neglected 形無視された　■delight 名楽しみ、喜び　■purity 純粋[純潔]であること　■moral worth 道徳的価値　■ladder はしご、踏み台　■deny oneself 自制する

男性の理想像だけが、女性の理想像のお手本だと考えられていたわけではない。それはまったくの誤解だ。日々の暮らしのなかで上品に振舞うことも求められた。音楽や舞踊、そして文学のたしなみも、なおざりにはされなかった。日本の文学史上、もっともすぐれた詩歌のいくつかは女性が詠ったものだ。日本舞踊（芸者の踊りのことではない）を教わるのは、動作を優雅に見せるためだ。音楽は、疲れた父親や夫を楽しませるためだった。芸術を学ぶことが目的ではなかった。もっと言えば、音楽の目的は、心の邪念を振り払うという崇高なものだった。音が澄んでいれば、心も澄んでいるといわれた。ここにも、若者の教育について述べたときの考え方が表れている。すなわち、大事なのは技術よりも道徳観ということだ。音楽や舞踊は、生活を優雅にし、明るくする。自分の能力を自慢するためではないのだ。

　日本の女性が習い事をするのも、見せびらかしたり、出世したりするためではなかった。家庭での娯楽として、家族や客人をもてなした。家庭生活が女性の教育の指針であった。彼女たちは家の名誉のために生き、懸命に働いた。娘として父のために、妻として夫のために、母として子のために、女性は自分を犠牲にした。幼いときから誰かのために生きることを教わった。女性の人生は自立したものではなく、誰かに従い、奉仕するものだった。こんな話は珍しくない。ひとりの若者が若い娘に恋をして両想いになった。だが若者が娘にばかり気をとられて、日ごろの務めをないがしろにするようになり、それに気づいた娘はわざと自分を醜くみせるようにした。娘に向けられた興味を、務

to those things he has to do. Azuma, the ideal wife in the minds of samurai girls, is loved by a man who is planning to kill her husband. She is able to take the place of her husband in the dark and the sword of the killer comes down on her own head. Another case is that of the wife of a young *daimyō*. She wrote a letter before taking her own life:

"I believe in fate. All is planned even before we are born. Only two short years ago we were eternally wed. I have followed you like a shadow follows an object. We are bound together, heart to heart, loving and being loved, never to part. I have learned, though, that the coming battle is to be your last. This is my farewell greeting to you. Why should I remain without you? I have no other hope or joy. I should rather wait for you on the road which all mortals must sometime take. Never, please, never forget the many benefits which our good master Hideyori has given you. The thanks we owe him is as deep as the sea and as high as the hills."

■eternally 副永久に　■bound 動bind（縛る、結びつける）の過去分詞形
■farewell 形別れの　■greeting 名挨拶の言葉、挨拶状　■mortals 名（死ぬ運命にある）人間　■benefit 名恩恵、利益

めに向けさせるためである。武士の娘にとって理想の妻である「吾妻*」
という女性は、夫を殺そうとたくらむ男から思いを寄せられていた。
吾妻は暗闇に乗じて夫の身代わりとなり、ふりおろされた暗殺者の剣
を自らの首に受けた。ある若い大名*の妻の例もある。彼女は自害の前
に、手紙を残した。

「私は運命というものを信じております。すべてはみな生まれる
前より定まっていたこと。私たちが夫婦となってまだわずか二年足
らずではございますが、影が物に寄り添うように、あなたについて
参りました。私たちはしっかりと固く結ばれ、お互いに相手を想い
あっており、離れ離れになることなど考えられません。ただ、聞く
ところによりますと、最後の戦に臨まれるとのこと。この手紙はお
別れのご挨拶です。あなたのいない世におめおめと生き残ることは
できません。他に望みも喜びもありません。むしろお先に死出の旅
路とやらで、あなたをお待ちしたほうがよいと思います。ご主君の
秀頼様からの多大なるご恩を決して決してお忘れのないよう。それ
は海のように深く、山のように大きいのですから」

*吾妻　北面の武士・渡辺左衛門尉渡の妻。袈裟御前として知られる。夫の同僚、遠藤盛遠（のちの文覚上人）
　に懸想され、遠藤は袈裟の母を脅し強引に思いを遂げようとする。思い悩んだ袈裟は遠藤に夫を殺すよう持ち
　かけ、その身代わりとなって死んだ。（『源平盛衰記』）
*ある若い大名　豊臣家の重臣、木村重成（1593-1615）のこと。大坂夏の陣で戦死。その妻青柳は大坂七手
　組頭・真野豊後守頼包の娘で、重成の死の1年後に自害したといわれている。

A woman gave herself willingly for the good of her husband, home and family. In the same way a man willingly gave himself for the good of his lord and country. She was not a slave of her husband and he was not a slave of his lord. The part she played was recognized as *naijo* (the inner help). Woman served man, man served lord, and the lord obeyed Heaven. It differs from Christianity in that this Western teaching requires each person to be directly responsible to the Creator. But both Bushido and Christianity teach that one should serve a cause higher than one's own self. Both are therefore based on eternal truth.

I am not excessively in favor of giving up one's own will. I also accept a lot of what Hegel said. He believed that history is the unfolding and realization of freedom. But the point I want to make is that self-sacrifice was completely and deeply planted in Bushido. It was required not only of women but also of men. So until this belief disappears, our society will not be ready for the American women's liberation demand: "May all the daughters of Japan rise in revolt against ancient customs!" Can such a revolt succeed? Will the rights they gain be worth losing their sweetness of character, their gentleness of manner? These and others are serious questions. Let us see if the status of women was so bad as to justify revolt.

In Japan there were about 2 million samurai. Above them were the military nobles, the *daimyō*, and the court nobles, the *kuge*.

■one's own self 自分自身　■excessively 副 過剰に　■unfold 動 (折り畳まれていたものが) 開く　■self-sacrifice 名 自己犠牲　■liberation 名 解放、自由化　■revolt 動 反抗する　■gain 動 得る

女性は、夫のため、家のため、家族のために喜んで自分の身を投げ出した。男性が主君や国のために喜んで身を投げ出すのと同じだった。だからといって妻が夫の奴隷でないのは、夫が主君の奴隷ではないのと一緒である。妻の役割は「内助」、すなわち家庭内の助けとして認められていた。女性が男性に仕え、男性が主君に仕え、そして主君は天に仕えた。その点、キリスト教とは異なっていて、この西洋の教えは、おのおのが創造主に直接の責任を負うことを説く。しかし武士道もキリスト教も、人は自分を捨て、より崇高な目的に仕えるべきだと教えている。したがって、武士道もキリスト教も永遠の真理にもとづいているのだ。

　私は、自分の意志を手放すことを必要以上に持ち上げているわけではない。ヘーゲルの言葉をおおかた受け入れてもいる。歴史は自由の展開と実現だとヘーゲルは考えていた。だが、ここではっきりさせたいのは、自己犠牲の精神は武士道に深く根づいているということだ。それは女性だけでなく、男性にとってもなくてはならないものだった。よって、この信念が消えてなくならないうちは、アメリカの女性解放運動が要求する「日本女性は全員、古臭い習慣に立ち上がって反抗せよ！」というスローガンに日本の社会は応えられないだろう。そんな反抗は成功するだろうか。気立ての良さや、たおやかな振る舞いを失ってまで、権利を勝ち取る価値はあるのだろうか。これら一切がはなはだ疑問である。反抗しても仕方ないほど女性の地位が低かったのかどうかをこれから見ていこう。

　日本には、およそ200万人の武士がいた。彼らの上には軍事貴族の

Those people enjoyed a life of luxury and were fighters in name only. Below them were the masses—the farmers, the craftsmen and the merchants. Spencer said that in a militant society the position of women is low. It improves only as society becomes more industrial. Another philosopher, Guizot, thought that feudalism and chivalry brought good influences. What Spencer said in regard to the low position of women may be said to have been confined to the samurai class. The industrial type applied to the classes above and below the samurai class. Samurai women had the least freedom. The lower the class, the more equal was the position of husband and wife. Among the higher nobility also there was not so much difference. So Spencer's thoughts were fully displayed in Old Japan. In regard to Guizot, he was thinking mostly of the higher nobility. So his idea applies to the *daimyō* and the *kuge*.

This is not to say that people had a low opinion of the status of women under Bushido. She was not treated as a man's equal. But until we learn to separate "difference" and "inequality" there will always be misunderstandings on this subject.

There are very few ways in which men are equal among themselves. Equality has no reference to mental or physical gifts from God. Men are equal only in terms of legal rights before the law. If that were the only measure, it would be easy to tell where a woman stands. But the question is whether or not there is a correct standard

■luxury 名ぜいたく ■improve 動改善する ■confine 動限定する ■nobility 名貴族 ■display 動～を表示する ■reference 名関連性 ■in terms of ～の観点から

「大名」と、宮廷貴族の「公家」がいた。大名も公家も贅沢な暮らしを送り、武人といっても名ばかりだった。武士の下には大衆——農民、職人、商人がいた。軍事社会においては女性の地位が低く、それが改善するのは産業がさかんな社会になったときだけだ、とスペンサー*は述べた。別の哲学者、ギゾー*は、封建制度と騎士道は良い影響を与えると考えた。女性の地位と言う点では、スペンサーの言う軍事社会は、武士という階級にのみあてはまり、産業のさかんな社会は、公家と農工商の階級にあてはまった。武家の女性には自由というものがほとんどなかった。階級が低くなればなるほど、夫婦の地位は、より対等になった。身分の高い貴族の間でも、そんなに違いはない。よって、旧日本においては、スペンサーの考え方の例えがいくらでもあった。ギゾーの説については、身分の高い貴族を対象にしていた。よって彼の考えは、大名や公家にあてはまる。

これは別に、武士道のもとでは女性の地位が軽んじられていたと言っているのではない。たしかに男性と対等には扱われなかった。しかし、「差異」と「不平等」の区別をつけるようにしなければ、この問題にはつねに誤解がつきまとうだろう。

男性の間でも平等であるのは、ほとんどまれだ。平等というのは、神から与えられた精神的あるいは肉体的能力とはなんの関係もない。法律の下での法的な権利だけが平等なのだ。もしも法が唯一のものさしならば、女性の地位がどの位置なのかはすぐにわかるだろう。だが問題は、正しい判断基準というものがあるのかどうか、ということであ

*ハーバート・スペンサー（1820-1903）　イギリスの哲学者、社会学者、倫理学者。明治期の日本ではスペンサーの著作が数多く翻訳され、読まれた。
*フランソワ・ギゾー（1787-1874）　フランスの歴史家、政治家。七月革命（1830）後政権を握るが、二月革命（1848）を招き失脚、イギリスへ亡命した。著書に『イギリス革命史』『ヨーロッパ文明史』など。

by which to judge. We cannot compare silver and gold. The most important standard is that which is within each person. It has to be a multiple standard. Bushido had its own standard, which consisted of two parts. One was the value of a woman on the battlefield, which was very little. The other was her value at home, which was very important. It was a double measurement. As a social-political unit, the woman was not counted for much. But as wife and mother she received the highest respect and deepest affection. For the Romans it was the same. Men bowed before women not as fighters or law-makers but as mothers. In Japan, fathers and husbands were absent in field or camp. The women were at home educating and caring for the young. The warlike exercises of women which I mentioned were mostly for the sake of educating their children.

Some foreigners have a superficial idea about what we think of our wives. A common Japanese expression for one's wife is "my rustic wife." So they think we do not hold her in high regard. But when we tell them we also use such words as "my foolish father," "my swinish son," "my clumsy self," isn't the answer clear enough?

To me it seems that our idea of union in marriage goes in some ways farther than the Christian notion. Western individual think-ing is that husband and wife are two persons, that they have separate rights and so on. It sounds strange to our ears when a husband or wife speaks of his or her partner as being kind, etc. We think praising

■multiple 形 多様な　■measurement 名 測定　■affection 名 愛情　■absent 形 不在の　■warlike 形 軍事の、戦争の　■rustic 形 野暮な、不作法な　■swinish 形 豚のような　■clumsy 形 不体裁な、出来の悪い

る。銀と金を比べることはできない。最も重要な基準は、各人のなかにある。それは多様な基準でなければならない。武士道には独自の基準があり、二つの項で成り立っていた。ひとつは戦場における女性の価値で、ほとんど評価されなかった。もうひとつは家庭における価値で、こちらは重要視された。つまり二重の評価だ。社会的・政治的な単位としては女性の地位は重くないが、妻や母としては最上級の尊敬と深い愛情を受けた。ローマ人にとっても、それは同じだった。男性が女性の前に身をかがめるのは、彼女たちが戦士や立法者だからではなく、母だからであった。日本では、父や夫が戦場に出て不在がちなとき、家にいる女性が子供たちを世話し、教育した。前に説明したように、女性が武芸の稽古をするのも、もっぱら子供たちの教育のためであることが多かった。

　外国人のなかには、日本人女性の地位について、表面的な見方しかしない者もいる。ふだん日本人は自分の妻を「荊妻（荊のかんざしをつけているような拙い妻）」と呼ぶ。だから日本の女性は尊敬されていないのだと考えるらしい。しかし、「愚父」「豚児」「拙者」などという言葉も使うことを教えてやれば、それで答えは十分だろう。
　日本人の結婚観は、ある意味でキリスト教徒の結婚観よりも進んでいるように私は思う。西洋の個人主義の考え方では、夫と妻は別々の人格であり、それぞれ別個の権利を持つ。夫や妻が自分の配偶者のことを優しいとかなんとか言うのは、日本人には奇妙に聞こえる。自分の妻をほめるのは、自分自身をほめるのと同じと考えるからだ。日本

one's own wife is praising a part of one's own self. Self-praise is regarded as bad taste among us, and I hope among Christian nations also. This is why we speak of "my rustic wife" etc.

The ancient Germanic men thought that their women were mysterious and unknowable. They regarded them with a mixture of wonder and fear. The Americans did not have enough women in the early days when the country was being settled. Those women, therefore, were highly valued, but not now. So the respect that man pays to woman in the West has become the chief standard of morality. But in the ethics of Bushido the dividing line between good and bad was different. It was located along the line of duty. This duty bound man to his own divine soul, and then to other souls in the five relations mentioned earlier in this book. Of these I have brought to your attention loyalty, the relation between one man as follower and another as lord. I have also touched upon the others as we went along in a more casual way because they were not characteristic of Bushido. Those others were based on natural feelings which could be common to all of mankind. They included the strong and tender friendship between man and man. Many stories could be told of the mutual loyalty between two men.

It is not surprising that the virtues and teachings unique to Bushido spread beyond the military class. We now must consider the influence of Bushido on the nation as a whole.

■unknowable 形 不可知の　■be settled 決着がつく　■divine 形 神聖な
■casual 形 形だけの　■characteristic 名 特性　■mutual 形 相互の　■as a whole 全
体として

人の間では、自画自賛は悪趣味とみなされているし、キリスト教徒の間でもそうあってほしいものだ。だから日本人は妻のことを「荊妻」などと呼ぶのである。

　ゲルマン民族は女性を神秘的でよくわからないものと考えていた。驚異と恐れの入り混じった目で女性を見た。アメリカは国の初期のころ、女性の数が少なかった。そのため、女性は大切にされた（だが今はそうでもない）。よって、西洋においては女性への敬意が、道徳の主な基準になった。だが、武士道の倫理観では、善と悪の境界線は別物だった。それは義務の道筋に沿って存在した。この義務が、人の内面にある崇高な魂と他の人の魂を、この本のはじめのほうで触れた五倫の道によって結びつけた。この五倫のうち、私は忠義——臣下と主君の関係について、注意をうながしておいた。他のことにも触れたが、あくまでも軽く触れただけで、なぜならそれらは武士道の特性とはいえないからだった。自然の感情に基づいたもので、全人類に共通のものといえる。そのなかには、男同士の強固で心のこもった友情がある。お互いの友情に忠実な二人の男の物語はいくらでもありそうだ。

　武士道に特有の徳と教えが、武士の階級をとびこえて広がったことは驚くにあたらない。そろそろ武士道が国民全体におよぼした影響を考察してみよう。

Chapter 15

The Influence of Bushido

So far we have looked only at a few of the high points of Bushido. Those were different from the general level of our national life. Like the sun spreading its light, the ethical system of the warrior class attracted followers from among the masses during the course of time. Virtues and vices alike spread from man to man.

The spread of liberty among the Anglo-Saxons hardly ever sprang from the masses. It was rather the work of a few gentlemen or nobles. Unfortunately, there was no gentleman in Eden. Adam and Eve paid a high price for his absence. If he had been there, they would have learned without painful experience that to disobey Jehovah is disloyal and dishonorable.

■so far 今までのところ ■high point 見せ場 ■course of time 時間の経過
■vice 名 悪徳 ■spring from ～から生じる ■pay a high price for ～に大きな代償
を支払う ■disobey 動 服従しない ■disloyal 形 不誠実な

第15章

武士道の影響

　これまで私たちは、武士道の肝心な部分をいくつか拾ってきたにすぎない。それらは国民生活の一般的なレベルとは違っていた。太陽の光が広がるように、武士階級の倫理体系はやがて大衆の間に広がっていった。美徳も悪徳も同様に人から人へ広がった。

　アングロ・サクソンの自由も広がっていったが、大衆から広がっていったことはほとんどなかった。むしろ、それは貴族やジェントルマンの業績だった。残念なことに、エデンの園にはジェントルマンは存在しなかった。おかげでアダムとイブは高い代価を払うことになった。もしもエデンの園にジェントルマンがいたら、アダムとイブは辛い目にあわずに、エホバに背くことは不忠かつ不名誉なことだと学んでいただろう。

What Japan was she owed to the samurai. They were not only the flower of the nation but its root as well. All the wonderful gifts of Heaven flowed through them. They kept themselves apart from the masses. But they set a moral standard and guided them by their example. In Europe the knights were a small part of the population. However, they occupied about one half of the drama in the literature. The same was true of Japan. The common people never tired of repeating the stories of Yoshitsune and his faithful follower Benkei; or the stories of the two brave Soga brothers. The tales of Nobunaga and Hideyoshi were told far into the night. Very young children heard the adventures of Momotaro, the hero who conquered the land of giants.

The samurai grew to represent the ideal beauty of the whole race. The people sang, "As among flowers the cherry is queen, so among men the samurai is lord." Every kind of thought, even business activities in which they did not take part, was influenced by Bushido.

It has been said that social progress is the unintended result of the actions of great men; also that it is a struggle of the few to lead the many in the best way. These things are true to a large degree of the part played by Bushido in Japan. The spirit of Bushido also spread to all classes by a certain kind of man known as *otoko-date* (one who protects the underdog). They were the natural leaders of democracy. They were very trustworthy men, every part of them

■occupy 動 占有する　■conquer 動 ～を制圧[征服]する　■progress 名 発達、進歩
■unintended 形 意図されたものではない　■underdog 名 敗残者、弱者
■trustworthy 形 信頼できる

昔の日本があるのは、武士のおかげであった。彼らは国の花だっただけではなく、国の根でもあった。すべての天の賜り物は彼らを通してもたらされた。武士は、大衆とは一線を引いていたが、彼らに道徳の基準を示し、自らが模範となって彼らを導いた。ヨーロッパでは、騎士は少数派にすぎなかった。しかし、文学においては騎士の物語が戯曲の半分を占めた。日本も同じだった。民衆は義経と忠臣弁慶*の物語や、勇敢な曾我兄弟*の物語を飽きずにくり返し語った。信長と秀吉の話は夜遅くまで語られた。幼子も、鬼が島で鬼退治をした桃太郎の冒険談を耳にした。

　武士は日本民族の理想美を体現するようになった。「花は桜木、人は武士」と人々は詠った。あらゆる思想、そして武士が関らない商業行為でさえ、武士道の影響を受けた。

　「社会の進化は、偉大な人間の行動が意図せず引き起こした結果である」と言われてきた。また、それは「選ばれた少数派の人々が、大衆を最善の方法で導こうとする奮闘」によってなされるとも言われた。これらのことは、日本において武士道が果たした役割の大半に当てはまっている。武士道の精神もまた、「男伊達（弱きを助ける人物）」として知られたある種の人物によって、すべての階級に広がった。彼らは民衆から自然に生まれたリーダーたちだった。頼りがいがあり、全身に豪

*義経と忠臣武蔵坊弁慶　平安末・鎌倉初期の僧、弁慶（?-1189）は、武勇を好み、のち武将源義経（1159-1189）に仕えた。2人の伝説は『義経記』『平家物語』などによって伝えられ、能や歌舞伎、浄瑠璃などでさまざまに脚色された。

*曾我兄弟　鎌倉初期の武士、曾我祐成（1172-1193）とその弟の時致（1174-1193）は、富士裾野の狩場で父の敵、工藤祐経（?-1193）を討つが、まもなく捕らえられ殺された。のちに『曾我物語』の題材となった。

strong with the strength of massive manhood. They were the spokesmen and guardians of popular rights. Each of them had a following of hundreds or thousands of people who offered loyalty and their very lives to their leaders, in the same way that the samurai did for the *daimyō*. Backed by a huge number of reckless working men, these natural-born "bosses" formed a strong check to the aggressive rise of the two-sworded class.

In many ways Bushido spread out to the other classes, providing a moral standard for all people. Even though the common man could not rise to the moral height of the *bushi*, their code came to represent the *Yamato Damashii* (the Soul of Japan). Matthew Arnold said that religion is "Morality touched by emotion." If that is so, Bushido should be called a religion. Motoori put the silent feeling of the nation into words when he wrote:

"Blessed isles of Japan! If strangers seek to know your Yamato spirit, tell them it is the sweet smell in the morning air, the fragrance of the wild cherry blossoms!"

■massive 形 圧倒的な、巨大な ■manhood 名 男らしさ ■guardian 名 保護者、守護者 ■reckless 形 向こう見ずな ■code 名 行動規範 ■blessed 形 聖なる ■isle 名 島

快な男らしさをしめす力がみなぎっていた。民衆の権利の代弁者であり、保護者であった。それぞれが数百、数千の子分を抱え、子分たちは、武士と大名のように、リーダーに忠誠と命を捧げた。天性の「親分」たちは大多数のむこうみずな労働者の支持を受け、武士階級が過度に台頭しないように目を光らせた。

　武士道はさまざまな方法で他の階級に広まり、すべての人々に道徳の基準を示した。平民の道徳は、武士の道徳の高みには追いつかなかったが、彼らの掟は「大和魂」をあらわすようになった。マシュー・アーノルドは、宗教が「感情に動かされた道徳」であると述べた。もしそうであれば、武士道は宗教といえるだろう。本居宣長＊は、国民の物言わぬ感情を言葉にした。

　　　　敷島の大和心を人間はば
　　　　朝日に匂ふ山桜花
　　　　　（日本人の心とは何かと尋ねられたら、
　　　　　　　朝日に映える山桜の花だと答えよう）

＊**本居宣長**（1730-1801）　江戸中期の国学者。医師を開業する傍ら、日本の古典研究に努めた。著書に『古事記伝』『源氏物語玉の小櫛』など。

Yes, the *sakura* has long been the favorite of our people and the symbol of our character. Note the word "wild." The Yamato spirit is wild in the sense of natural growth. It is natural to the soil. The elegance and grace of its beauty appeal to us as no other flower can. The rose has showy colors and strong smells. The flower decays on the stem. These things are very unlike our flower. The colors are never gorgeous; it has no thorns hidden under its beauty; one never tires of its fragrance and it is always ready to die at the call of nature. When the delicious perfume of the *sakura* refreshes the morning air, few sensations are more wonderful than to take in the very breath of a beautiful day.

The Creator Himself is said to have made new resolutions in His heart upon smelling a sweet fragrance. So is it any wonder that the sweet-smelling season of the cherry blossom should arouse the whole nation? At that time, for a while, they can forget their tiredness and their sorrows. After their brief pleasure, they return to their work with new strength and new resolutions. So the *sakura* is the flower of the nation in more ways than one.

This sweet flower goes with the wind and leaves its fragrance behind, ready to disappear forever. Is it the type of the Yamato spirit? Is the soul of Japan so weakly mortal?

■showy 形 人目を引く　■decay 動 朽ちる　■gorgeous 形 豪華な、華やかな
■thorn 名 とげ　■call of nature 自然の求め　■perfume 名 香り　■resolution 名
決心、決意

そう、桜は昔からずっと日本人の愛する花であり、日本人の国民性の象徴だった。とくに「山桜」という言葉に注目してほしい。自生の植物という点で、大和魂は山桜である。わが国の土壌に根づいているからだ。その上品で優雅な美しさは、他のどんな花もかなわないほど、日本人の心に訴えかける。バラは色が派手で、匂いもきつい。花は茎の先で朽ちてゆく。日本の桜とは似ても似つかない。桜の色は決して華美ではなく、美の下にとげを隠したりせず、香りはほのかで、自然が呼びかければいつでもその命を捨てる覚悟がある。そのかぐわしい香りが朝の大気を清めるとき、美しい一日の息吹を吸い込むことほど、すばらしい気分を感じることはない。

　創造主自身が、甘い香りを嗅いで、新たな決意を固めたと言われている。そうであるならば、桜の花が甘く香る季節に全国民が浮き足立つのも無理はない。そんなとき、日ごろの疲れや悲しみを少しの間は忘れることができるのだ。短い間の楽しみごとが終わると、彼らは新たな力と新たな決心とともに仕事場へ戻る。だから、桜はあらゆる意味で国民の花である。
　桜は風に吹かれ、甘い香りを残し、永遠に消えようとする。では、これが大和魂の典型なのだろうか。日本の魂は、そんなにはかなく滅びるものなのだろうか。

Chapter 16

Is Bushido Still Alive?

Has Western civilization, in its march through our land, already destroyed every trace of Bushido? It would be very sad if a nation's soul could die so fast.

The various things which go into the making of national character are very tough and are not given up easily. They are like the parts of animals that cannot be reduced any further (the fins of a fish, the beak of a bird, the teeth of a meat-eating animal). It has been said that the intelligent discoveries are the common heritage of humanity; also that good and bad points of character are the exclusive heritage of each people. Each national character is unique. However, in studying the various virtues of Bushido, we have looked at European sources for comparison. We have seen that not one quality of character was exclusive to Bushido. The total of moral qualities which unite the most powerful persons of every country is

■trace 跡、形跡　■reduce 動少なくする、減らす　■fin 名ヒレ　■beak 名くちばし　■heritage 名遺産　■exclusive 形唯一の、独占する　■unite 動結合する

第16章

武士道はまだ生きているか

　わが国に勢いよく押し寄せてきた西洋文明は、武士道の痕跡を破壊しつくしてしまったのか。一国民の魂がそれほどあえなく滅びてしまうのだとしたら、じつに悲しいことだ。

　国民性を形づくるさまざまな要素は、強固に結びつき、たやすく切り離せるものではない。それは、動物に欠くことのできない部分があるのと同じだ（魚のひれ、鳥のくちばし、肉食動物の牙のように）。これまで、知性による発見は全人類の遺産だといわれてきた。一方で、国民性の美点や欠点はそれぞれの国民固有の遺産だといわれてきた。国民性はその国ごとに違いがある。ところが、武士道のさまざまな徳目をヨーロッパの事例と比べてみると、武士道にしか見られない美点は１つもなかった。道徳的美点の集合体は、一国民だけが有する遺産ではなく、あらゆる国の最も有力な人々をつなぎ、互いに理解を深めさせるものだ。それは、正しい相手からはすぐに感じとることができる。武士道が日本人（とりわけサムライ）に刻みつけた性格はとても重要な

not the exclusive heritage of this nation or that nation. This total of moral qualities makes powerful people understandable and agreeable to each other. It is known at once if a person is "one of us."

The character which Bushido impressed on our nation (and on the samurai in particular) is a vital element. Bushido is not a physical force and it is not transmitted by heredity. It is rather an unconscious and irresistible power. It has been moving the nation and individuals for several hundred years. Bushido is not written down in a precise and systematic form. But it was and is the animating spirit, the engine of our country. It is said that there are three distinct forms of Japan in existence side by side today. These are the old which has not totally died out, the new (hardly born except in spirit) and the transitional which is now passing through its most critical pain and struggle. This is mostly true. But when it comes to basic ethical ideas, Bushido is still the guiding light of the transitional period and will prove to be the formative force of the new era.

■vital element 不可欠の要素　■heredity 名遺伝　■unconscious 形無意識の
■irresistible 形抵抗できない　■precise 形明確な　■side by side 並んで　■die out 廃れる　■transitional 形過渡期の

要素だ。武士道は物理的な力ではなく、遺伝で継承されるものではない。むしろ抗うことのできない無意識の力として、国民全体、そして一人ひとりを、数百年にわたって衝き動かしてきた。

　武士道は文書として形式的に定められてはいない。しかし昔も今も、人々に生気を与える活力であり、わが国のエンジンでありつづけている。今日、3つの日本が並んで存在しているといわれる。老いているがまだ死んではいない日本、かろうじて精神だけが生まれたばかりの日本、そして過渡期にあって最も激しい苦痛と闘っている日本。この見方はほぼ正しい。しかし、基本的な倫理概念として、武士道は今も過渡期の日本を導くともし火であり、新しい時代を形づくる力であるのは間違いない。

The great Restoration statesmen were men who knew no other moral teaching than that of Knighthood. Some writers have recently tried to prove that the Christian missionaries contributed quite a lot to the making of New Japan. I am ready to give honor to whom honor is due. But this honor cannot yet be recognized. As for me, I believe that the good missionaries are doing great things for Japan in education, especially moral education. But they have done little that we can see in forming the New Japan. No, it was Bushido, pure and simple, that urged us on. Look at the biographies of men like Sakuma, Saigo, Okubo, Kido, Ito, Okuma, Itagaki and others. You will see that it was samuraihood which was the maker of Modern Japan. Mr. Henry Norman, in his study of the Far East, said that the ruling influence among the people of Japan is the strictest, highest and most ceremonial code of honor that man has ever made.

■Restoration 名 明治維新　■statesman 名 指導的政治家　■missionary 名 宣教師
■contribute 動 貢献する　■strict 形 厳しい、厳格な　■code of honor 社交儀礼

明治維新に尽くした偉大な政治家たちは、道徳の教えといえば武士道しか知らなかった。最近、新しい日本の国づくりにキリスト教宣教師たちが大いに寄与したと証明しようとした著者が何人かいる。私は、名誉に値する人であれば喜んで称えたいと思う。だが、この件についてはそれに値するかまだ分からない。個人的には、優れた宣教師たちが日本の教育面、おもに道徳教育において大きな仕事を果たしていると思う。しかし新しい日本の国づくりに関しては、目に見える貢献はほとんどしていない。むしろ、日本人を駆り立てたのは、ほかでもない武士道そのものだった。佐久間象山*、西郷隆盛*、大久保利通*、木戸孝允*、伊藤博文*、大隈重信*、板垣退助*といった人々の回顧録を見てほしい。サムライの精神である武士道こそ、現代日本をつくりあげた力だと分かるはずだ。ヘンリー・ノーマン氏は、極東を研究したうえでこう述べている。日本の国民に浸透し影響を及ぼすその力は、人類史上、最も厳格で、高潔で、儀礼を重んじた名誉の掟であると。

*佐久間象山（1811-1864）　信濃松代藩士。開国論、公武合体論を主張し、攘夷派に暗殺される。
*西郷隆盛（1828-1877）　薩摩藩出身の軍人・政治家。薩長同盟の成立や王政復古に成功。西南戦争に敗れ、自刃。
*大久保利通（1830-1878）　薩摩藩出身の政治家。参議、大蔵卿、内務卿。
*木戸孝允（1833-1877）　長州藩出身の政治家。旧名桂小五郎。参議。
*伊藤博文（1841-1909）　長州藩出身の政治家。初代首相を務め、組閣4度に及ぶ。初代韓国統監。
*大隈重信（1838-1922）　佐賀藩出身の政治家。首相。
*板垣退助（1837-1919）　土佐藩出身の政治家。自由民権運動を指導。

The transformation of Japan is a fact which is clear to the world. There were various things behind it but if we have to name the main one, it was surely Bushido. We opened the whole country to foreign trade. We introduced the latest improvements in every part of life. We began to study Western politics and sciences. For all of those things the guiding light was not the development of our physical resources or the increase of wealth; much less was it a blind imitation of Western customs.

A close observer of Asian customs and peoples has said:

"We are told every day how Europe has influenced Japan. But we forget that the change there was totally self-generated. Europeans did not teach Japan. Japan of herself chose to learn from Europe methods of organization, civil and military, which have so far proved successful. She imported European science. That is not exactly influence, unless we can say that England is influenced by purchasing tea in China. Where is the teacher, the philosopher or statesman from Europe who has re-made Japan?"

■transformation 图変化、変質 ■improvement 图改善、向上 ■blind imitation of 〜のやみくも的な模倣 ■self-generated 形自然発生した、自発的な
■purchase 動購入する

日本の変化は世界から見ても明らかな事実だ。背景にはさまざまな要因があるが、あえて１つ挙げるならやはり武士道。私たちは日本全国を解放し外国と貿易をはじめた。生活のあらゆる面で、最新の改良を採り入れた。西洋の政治や科学を学びはじめた。こうした取り組みの動機となったのは、物的資源や富を増強させることでも、ましてや西洋の慣習を盲目的に真似ることでもなかった。

アジアの慣習や国民について詳しく研究したある評論家*はつぎのように述べている。

　　「われわれは、いかにヨーロッパが日本に影響を与えたかを日々聞かされている。だが、日本の変化はあくまで自発的なものであったことを忘れているようだ。ヨーロッパが日本に学ばせたのではない。日本が自ら選んで、ヨーロッパにおいて現状成功している体制や行政や軍の仕組みを学んだのだ。日本はヨーロッパの科学を輸入した。イギリスが茶を輸入したことで中国から影響されたと言うのでないかぎり、これは影響とは言えない。では、日本をつくり直したというヨーロッパの指導者や哲学者、政治家はどこにいるのか」

***ある評論家**　メレディス・タウンゼント（1831–1911）のこと。イギリスのジャーナリスト。

Mr. Townsend is right. If only he had looked into our psychology, he would easily have seen that the spring of our self-motivated action was no other than Bushido. The strongest motive was the sense of honor which cannot bear being looked down upon as an inferior power. Money or industrial reasons came later in the process of change.

 The influence of Bushido is very clear if you look into Japanese life through Lafcadio Hearn's writings. He was the most eloquent and truthful interpreter of the Japanese mind. The politeness of all of the people, derived from knightly ways, is very well known. The physical endurance, strength and bravery of the soldiers was shown in the Sino-Japanese war. Many people ask if there is any nation more loyal or patriotic. For the answer that there is not we must thank the teachings of Knighthood.

On the other hand, it is fair to recognize that for the faults and defects of our character, Bushido is also largely responsible. Some of our young men have already gained international fame in science but not in philosophy. This is because of a lack of such training in the education of Bushido. Our idea of honor is responsible for us being too sensitive and touchy. Some foreigners say we think too highly of ourselves; if so, that also is a problem resulting from honor.

■no other than ～に他ならない ■look down 見下ろす ■look into ～を詳しく調べる ■eloquent 形 雄弁な ■interpreter 名 解釈者 ■patriotic 形 愛国心の強い ■touchy 形 神経質な、気難しい ■think highly of ～を高く評価する

タウンゼント氏のこの意見は正しい。もし彼が日本人の心理を探求していれば、私たちの自発的な行動の源泉が武士道にほかならないことを簡単に突きとめただろう。日本人にとって何より強い動機となったのは、劣った勢力として見下されることに耐えられない名誉心だった。経済や産業上の動機は、変化の過程において後から生じたものだ。

　武士道の影響は、ラフカディオ・ハーン*が描いた日本の暮らしを見てもよく分かる。ハーンは、日本人の心の最も雄弁で忠実な解釈者だった。日本人がみな武士の流儀に由来する礼儀正しさを備えていることはよく知られている。日本兵の肉体的な忍耐力、強靭さ、そして勇敢さは、日清戦争で示された。日本人ほど忠誠心と愛国心のある国民がほかにいるだろうか、と問われることは多い。その問いに「いない」と答えられるのは、まさに武士道の教えのおかげだ。

　一方、日本人の欠点や短所についても武士道に大きな原因があることを認めねば公平ではないだろう。たとえば科学分野にはすでに国際的評価を得ている日本の若者もいるが、哲学の分野にはいない。それは、武士道の教育において哲学的思考の訓練が欠けていたためだ。また、日本人の繊細かつ激しやすい一面は、私たちの名誉観から生じるものだ。外国人のなかには日本人は自尊心が高すぎると言う人もいるが、その通りならば、それも強い名誉心のせいだろう。

*ラフカディオ・ハーン（1850-1904）　ギリシア生まれの新聞記者、随筆家、小説家。1890年に来日し、翌年日本人女性小泉節と結婚。日本に帰化し、小泉八雲として日本に関する多くの著作を残す。主な著書に『怪談』『心』など。

Have you seen in Japan many young men walking around the streets as if they don't care at all about worldly things? They have messy hair, ragged clothes and carry a large cane or a book. They are *shosei* (students), to whom the earth is too small and heaven is not high enough. They have their own ideas about everything. They live in castles in the clouds and feed on airy words of wisdom. Their eyes are filled with the fire of ambition and their minds are thirsty for knowledge. Being poor only serves to drive them onward harder; worldly goods only tie them down. They preserve loyalty and patriotism. They are the self-appointed guardians of national honor. With all of their virtues and faults, they are the last surviving remnants of Bushido.

Deep-rooted and powerful as is still the effect of Bushido, it is an unconscious and silent influence. The heart of the people responds to any appeal to what it has received from past tradition. The word "loyalty" revived all the noble feelings that were once strong but which had become weak. A group of students were out of control and on strike because of their dissatisfaction with a certain teacher at their college. Their strike was broken up by the Dean. He asked two simple questions: "Does your professor have a good character? If so, you should respect him and keep him in the school. Is he weak? If so, it is not manly to push a falling man." The problem with the professor became small compared to the moral issues. By arousing the feelings of Bushido, great moral renewal can be accomplished.

■ragged 形 みすぼらしい　■airy 形 実体のない　■ambition 名 野心、熱望
■onward 副 前方へ　■remnant 名 名残　■revive 動 よみがえらせる　■Dean 名 学部長　■accomplish 動 成し遂げる、果たす

日本を訪れた読者の方は、この世の俗事にはいかにも関心がなさそうに道を行く若者たちを見かけただろうか。髪を乱し、粗末な着物を身につけ、大きな杖か書物を抱えている。彼ら書生（学生）にとって、地球はあまりに小さく、天が高すぎることはない。万事について独自の考えを持っている。雲上の城に住み、知恵という言葉の泡を食す。その目は大志に燃え、心は知識を渇望する。貧しさはいっそう貪欲に前へ進むための刺激にすぎず、世俗的な物品は自分たちを縛りつけるものでしかない。彼らは忠誠心と愛国心を守り続け、国家の名誉の番人を自ら任じている。その美点も欠点もまとめて、彼らは武士道最後の名残りなのだ。

　武士道は今も深く根づき、大きな力を持っているが、その影響は意識されることも言葉にされることもない。日本人の心は、先祖から継承してきたものに訴えかけてくるものがあれば、何であれそれに応える。「忠義」という言葉は、かつての強さを失っていたあらゆる高貴な感情を甦らせた。ある大学では、学生の一団がある教師への不満を爆発させ、ストライキをおこした。ストライキを終わらせたのは学長だった。学長は２つの単純な問いを学生に投げかけた。「君たちの教授は立派な性格の持ち主か？　そうであるなら、教授を敬い、大学に留まってもらうことだ。教授は弱い人間か？　そうであるなら、倒れかけている人を押すのは男らしくない」。この道徳的な問いかけを前に、教授をめぐる騒動は些細なものとなった。武士道によって育まれた感情を呼び起こせば、道徳の偉大なる再生を果たすことができるのだ。

One reason why missionary work fails is because the people do not know about our history at all. Some do not care about our history. They separate their religion from the way of thinking we have had for many centuries. Ignoring our past, the missionaries say that Christianity is a new religion. But I think it is a very old story. It needs to be expressed in words which are familiar to the moral development of a people. Then it will easily find a place in their hearts, regardless of race or nationality. Christianity, as taught by modern missionaries, does not have the grace and purity of its Founder. It is therefore unsuitable for those brought up under the code of Bushido. The teachers of Christianity cannot uproot our traditions and plant their own ideas in our soil. Jesus Himself would never have thought of doing such a thing.

One wise man said that men have divided the world into Christian and non-Christian, without thinking about the good and bad in both. They have compared the best part of themselves with the worst part of their neighbors. They have not been fair. They have been satisfied to accumulate all that can be said in praise of their own and all that can be said to criticize others.

There are signs and fears that there are forces at work to threaten the future of Bushido.

■regardless 形 ～にかかわらず　■founder 名 創始者　■unsuitable 形 不適当な
■uproot 動 ～を根絶する　■criticize 動 批判する　■threaten 動 ～を脅す

キリスト教宣教の失敗の一因は、宣教師たちが日本の歴史をまったく知らないことにある。私たちの歴史にはまるで配慮しない宣教師もいる。彼らはキリスト教の信仰と、日本人が何百年も慣れ親しんできた考え方とを切り離そうとする。私たちの歴史を無視し、キリスト教は新しい宗教だと主張する。だが私が思うに、キリスト教は遥か古の物語だ。それを伝えるには、人々の道徳水準に照らして親しみやすい言葉で語るべきだ。そうすれば、人種も国籍も問わず、たやすく人々の心に届けられるだろう。現代の宣教師たちが説くキリスト教には、創造者の恩寵と純粋さが欠けている。そのため、武士道の掟がもたらした考え方とは相容れない。宣教師たちは、日本人の伝統を根こそぎにし、その地に彼らの新しい考え方を植え付けることはできない。イエスご自身が、決してそのような行いはなさらないはずだ。

　ある賢者はこう言った。人々は世界をキリスト教徒と異教徒とに分かち、たがいに善悪を併せ持つことを考えなかった。キリスト教徒は、自分たちの最善の部分と隣人の最悪の部分とを比べてきた。公平であろうとしなかった。そして自分たちの宗教に贈られうる称賛の言葉のみを、ほかの宗教に浴びせられる非難の言葉のみを集めて満足してきた。
　武士道の未来を脅かすさまざまな力が働いている、そんな兆候や不安が漂っている。

Chapter 17

The Future of Bushido

One can make a close comparison between the chivalry of Europe and the Bushido of Japan. If history repeats itself, the fate of the latter will be close to that of the former. The particular and local causes for the decay of chivalry in Europe do not apply much to Japanese conditions. But the larger and more general causes are working for the decline of Bushido.

One difference is that in Europe, when chivalry was detached from feudalism, it got a fresh start with support from the Church. But in Japan there was no religion large enough to nourish it. So, when Bushido found itself without its mother (feudalism), it was like an orphan which had to do everything by itself. Bushido did not fit with and had no support from modern military warfare, Shintoism or ancient Chinese wisdom. Other moral theories have been invented but they exist only in the newspapers.

■decline 動衰退する　■detach 動引き離す、取り外す　■fresh start 再出発
■orphan 名孤児　■warfare 名戦争行為

第17章

武士道の未来

　ヨーロッパの騎士道と日本の武士道は、詳しい比較を行うのに適した組み合わせだ。歴史は繰り返すとすれば、武士道は騎士道と同じような運命をたどるだろう。騎士道衰退の原因のうち、地域に由来する特殊なものは日本の状況にはあてはまらない。しかし、より広く一般的な原因については武士道の凋落にもあてはまる。

　1つ両者の大きな違いは、ヨーロッパの騎士道が、封建制度から切り離されたのちキリスト教会の支援を得て再出発した点だ。しかし日本には、武士道を支え養えるほど大規模な宗教はなかった。そのためいざ封建制度という母を失うと、武士道は孤児のごとく孤立無援になった。武士道は、現代的な軍事戦争や、神道、古代中国の思想とは相容れず、支援も得られなかった。ほかにも道徳理論は編み出されてきたが、どれも新聞上で語られるだけにすぎない。

Some countries and powers are set against the code of Knighthood. The ceremonial code has decayed into the low-level life of the industrial classes in the eyes of some people. Democracy does not tolerate the concentration of power in the hands of only one group. It was the only thing strong enough to swallow up what remained of Bushido. The present forces of society are against class spirit and chivalry is a class spirit. Modern society cannot recognize interests which are only for one class. Other modern things also make Bushido unsuitable for our times—the progress of popular instruction, of industrial arts and habits, of wealth and city life. The State built upon the rock of Honor is fast changing. Power is now in the hands of lawyers and politicians. The social structure in which the intense behavior of the samurai took shape is at the point of disappearing forever.

If history can teach us anything, a state built on warrior virtues can never continue. The fighting instinct in man is natural and universal but it does not represent the whole man. Beneath the instinct to fight there is a more sacred instinct to love. We have seen that Shinto, Mencius and Wan Yang Ming have all clearly taught us about this instinct to love. But Bushido and all other militant types of practical ethics, too often forgot to emphasize love. Things which are more noble and broader than the warrior's concerns claim our attention today. Life is bigger now. With this larger view, with the

■be set against ～に反発する ■tolerate 動許容する ■concentration 名集中
■swallow up 飲み込む ■take shape 形になる ■universal 形普遍の

さまざまな勢力や権威が、武士道の掟に抗おうとしている。産業階級において儀礼の掟は衰退し、生活が通俗化したと見る人もいる。民主主義はいかなる特権集団も許さない。民主主義だけでも、武士道の残滓を飲み込んでしまうほどの強い力がある。現代の社会的勢力は階級精神を嫌うが、武士道も階級精神の1つだ。現代社会は階級による利益の独占を認めない。このほかにも現代のさまざまな状況が、武士道を時代にそぐわないものにしている——普通教育の普及、産業技術や経済、都市生活の発展などがそうだ。名誉の岩の上に築かれた国家は急速に変わりつつある。今、力を持っているのは法律家や政治家だ。サムライの壮烈な振る舞いを育んだ社会構造は、このままでは永遠に消えてしまう。

　もし歴史から学べることがあるとすれば、それは武徳によって築かれた国家はけっして永続しないということだ。人間の闘争本能は自然で普遍的なものだが、人間全体を表すわけではない。闘争本能の下にはより神聖な、愛するという本能がある。これまで見てきたように、神道や孟子、王陽明はみな、この愛するという本能についてはっきりと説いている。しかし武士道をはじめとする軍事的な形態の倫理は、しばしば愛を重視することをおろそかにしてきた。闘士の使命よりも高潔で幅広い使命が今、日本人の関心を集めている。今日、人々の人生は広がりをみせている。視野が大きくなり、民主主義が台頭し、ほかの

growth of democracy, with better knowledge of other peoples and nations, the Confucian idea of goodness and the Buddhist idea of pity will expand. They will merge into the Christian idea of love. We are now more than subjects, more than citizens. We are men. We believe that the angel of peace will chase away the clouds of war. The prophecy that "the meek shall inherit the earth" is confirmed by the history of the world. A nation should cherish its birthright of peace. It should not shift from the front rank of industrialism to lawless militarism.

When the conditions of society are so changed that they have become not only opposite but also hostile to Bushido, it is time to prepare for an honorable funeral. It is as difficult to say when chivalry died as it is to say when it began. In Europe it is said that chivalry died in 1559 when Henry II of France was killed. In Japan feudalism was abolished in 1870, which was the funeral bell for Bushido. Five years later, it was prohibited to wear swords. This rang out the old and rang in the new age of economists, calculators and people who use clever arguments which are basically unsound.

■merge 動融合する ■prophecy 名預言 ■meek 名おとなしい人、柔和な人 ■hostile 形敵意を持った ■funeral 名葬儀 ■abolish 動廃止する ■prohibit 動禁止する ■unsound 形不安定な

民族や外国の知識が増すとともに、孔子の仁の思想や仏教の慈悲の思想が広がり、キリスト教の愛の思想と合わさり一つになるだろう。私たちは今や臣民以上の、いや市民以上の存在となった。私たちは人間なのだ。平和の天使が戦争の暗雲を追い払ってくれると信じよう。「優しき者は地を受け継ぐだろう」という預言が正しいことは、世界の歴史が証明している。国民は、平和という生まれもった権利を大切にすべきだ。けっして産業主義の前線から退き、無法な軍国主義に転向してはいけない。

　社会状況が大きく変わり、武士道と相反するどころか敵対するほどになった今、武士道の名誉にふさわしく葬るための準備をはじめるべきだ。騎士道が滅びた時期は、その誕生時期と同じくらい判断しがたい。ヨーロッパでは、フランスのアンリ2世*が殺された1559年に騎士道は廃止されたといわれている。日本では、1870年の封建制度の廃止が武士道の弔鐘を鳴らした。その5年後、刀の携帯が禁止された。これがきっかけで、鐘の音とともに古い時代は送り出され、経済家と打算家と詭弁家による新しい時代が迎えられた。

---

*アンリ2世（1519-1559）　フランス王。娘エリザベートとスペイン王フェリペ2世の結婚祝賀の馬上槍試合で、過失により重症を負い死亡する。

It has been said that Japan won her recent war with China by means of Murata guns and the Krupp cannon; or it has been said that the victory was the work of a modern school system. But these are less than half-truths. Does a piano, even of the best workmanship such as Ehrbar or Steinway, suddenly make the sounds of the Rhapsodies of Liszt or the Sonatas of Beethoven without a master's hand? No, it is the spirit of man which stimulates action, no matter what tools we have to work with. The most improved guns and cannons do not shoot by themselves; the most modern educational system does not make a hero out of a coward. No! What won the battles on the Yalu, in Korea and Manchuria, were the spirits of our fathers. They were guiding our hands and beating in our hearts. The spirits of our warlike ancestors are not dead. To those who have eyes to see, they are clearly visible. Look under the skin of a Japanese with the most advanced ideas and you will see a samurai. The great inheritance of honor, valor and all warrior virtues is for us to guard, to cherish. We should make sure that the ancient spirit is not diminished. The command of the future is such that the application of that spirit will be widened in scope to all aspects and relations of life.

■cannon 名大砲 ■half-truth 名半端な真実 ■stimulate 動刺激する ■no matter what たとえ何があろうと ■improved 形改良された ■command 名命令、指令 ■scope 名（行動・思考などの）範囲、領域

近年の中国との戦争（日清戦争）における日本の勝因は、村田銃とクルップ砲*だといわれている。あるいは、近代的な学校教育制度のおかげだともいわれている。だがこれらは真実の半分にも満たない。たとえばピアノは、エルバーやスタインウェイ*が手がけた一流の名器だとしても、優れた弾き手なくしてリスト*のラプソディやベートーヴェン*のソナタをひとりでに奏でるだろうか。いや、人間の精神こそが行動を促すのであり、それはどんな道具を扱おうとも変わらない。最新鋭の銃も大砲も、自ら発射することはできない。最先端の教育制度も、臆病者を英雄にしたてることはできない。できるはずがない！　鴨緑江や朝鮮、満州での戦いに勝利をもたらしたのは、私たちの父祖の霊魂だった。それは私たちの心のなかで脈打ち、行く手を導いてくれた。勇ましい父祖の霊魂は今も死んではいない。見る目を持つ人には、はっきりと見えるはずだ。最も進んだ思想を持つ日本人の皮を剥げば、なかからサムライの姿が現れるだろう。名誉や勇気といったすべての武徳の偉大なる遺産を、私たちは大切に守らねばならない。古来の精神を薄れさせてはならない。この使命を将来果たしていくには、その精神を活かす場面を広げ、生活のあらゆる場面で採り入れることだ。

*村田銃とクルップ砲　村田銃は日本初の国産小銃で、日清戦争では13年式が使用された。クルップ砲はドイツのクルップ社が発明した鋳鋼の砲。
*エルバーやスタインウェイ　エルバーはオーストリアの、スタインウェイはドイツのピアノメーカー。いずれのピアノも名器といわれる。
*フランツ・リスト（1811–1886）　ハンガリー生まれの作曲家、ピアノ演奏者。
*ルートヴィヒ・ヴァン・ベートーヴェン（1770–1827）　ドイツの作曲家。

It has been predicted that the moral system of feudal Japan will crumble into dust. It is also predicted that a new system of ethics will rise to lead the New Japan in her path of progress. Desirable and probable as this prediction is, the New Japan must come from within, not from the outside. "The Kingdom of God is within you." It does not come rolling down the mountains, no matter how grand it is. It does not come sailing across the seas, no matter how wide. The Koran says that God has given every people a prophet in its own language. The seeds of the Kingdom blossomed in Bushido. Now the days of Bushido are coming to a close. We look everywhere for other sources of sweetness and light, of strength and comfort. But as of yet nothing has been found to take its place. The profit-and-loss philosophy of practical materialists is popular among people with half a soul. The only other ethical system which is strong enough to successfully manage that practical materialism is Christianity. Like the Hebrew prophets who came before Christ (in particular Isaiah, Jeremiah, Amos and Habakkuk), Bushido put special stress on the moral conduct of rulers, public men and nations. But the ethics of Christ stresses individuals and His personal followers. This will find more practical application as individualism grows stronger.

■predict 動 ～を予測する　■crumble 動 粉々に崩れる　■no matter how どんなに ～であろうとも　■prophet 名 預言者　■blossom 動 開花する　■materialist 名 唯物 主義者

封建時代の日本の道徳体系は崩れて塵と化すといわれてきた。また、新たな倫理体系が生まれ、新しい日本を進歩へ導くだろうともいわれてきた。こうした預言の実現は望ましいし、起こりうることだが、新しい日本はあくまで内から立ち現れるものであり、外から現れるものではない。「神の王国は汝らの内にある*」。神の王国は、いかに山が高くとも、その上から降りてくるものではない。いかに海が広くとも、その向こうから渡ってくるものではない。コーランには、神はすべての民族にその国の言葉で話す預言者を与えた、とある。神の王国の種は、武士道のなかで花開いた。しかし今や、武士道の時代は終わりを迎えつつある。私たちは、優美さと光の源、力強さと慰めの源となるべつの何かをいたるところに探し求めている。しかし、いまだ武士道に代わるものは見つかっていない。唯物主義者らの損得勘定の哲学が、魂を半分なくした人々のあいだで好まれている。唯物論に十分対抗できる力のある倫理体系は、キリスト教だけだ。イエス・キリスト以前のヘブライの預言者たち（とりわけイザヤ、エレミヤ、アモス*、ハバクク*ら）のように、武士道は支配者や公職者、国民の道徳的な行いを重視した。一方、キリスト教の倫理は、個人そしてキリストを個人的に信奉する者を重視している。個人主義の勢いが増すにしたがい、キリスト教の倫理は実生活でもさらに適用されていくだろう。

＊「神の王国は汝らのなかにあり」　新約聖書『ルカによる福音書』第17章21節より。また、ロシアの作家トルストイ（1828-1910）の作品名。
＊アモス　旧約聖書『アモス書』を書いたとされるテコアの牧者（同書1-1）。
＊ハバクク　旧約聖書『ハバクク書』を書いたとされる人物（同書1-1）。

Christianity and practical materialism will divide the world between them. Lesser systems of morals will join either side for their preservation. Which side will Bushido join? Like the cherry blossom, it is willing to die with the first wind of the day. But it will probably never disappear completely. The teaching that virtue is the highest good may be dead as a system. But virtue itself is alive. It is felt in various ways of life, in the philosophy of Western nations and in the laws in all of the civilized world. No, whenever man struggles to raise himself above himself, whenever his spirit masters his flesh by his own efforts, there we see the immortal discipline of virtue at work.

Bushido as an independent code of ethics may disappear, but not its power. Its particular ways of thinking about the warrior or honor may be destroyed. But its light and glory will continue thereafter for a long time. Like its symbolic flower, after it is blown in all directions by the winds, Bushido will still bless mankind with its perfume. It will enrich life. Long after, when its practices have been buried and its very name forgotten, its aromas will come floating in the air, as from a distant, unseen hill.

■preservation 图保存 ■civilized 形文明化した ■bless 動〜を祝福する
■enrich 動豊かにする ■aroma 名香り

キリスト教と唯物論は世界を二分するだろう。これらより小さい道徳体系が生き残るためには、いずれかの側につかねばならない。武士道はどちらを選ぶのか。桜の花のように、武士道はその日最初の風に吹かれて散っていくかもしれない。しかし、完全に消え失せはしないだろう。徳は最高の善であるという武士道の教えは、倫理体系としては滅んだかもしれない。だがその徳そのものは今も生きている。それは人生のさまざまな場面で、西洋諸国民の哲学やあらゆる文明世界の法において、感じとることができる。それだけではない。人が自らを超えようと闘うとき、人が努力によって精神で肉体を支配するときはいつでも、ゼノン*の不滅の教訓が働いていることがわかる。

　武士道は、1つの独立した倫理の掟としては消滅するかもしれないが、その力が消え去ることはない。独特な武勇と名誉の流儀は廃れてしまうかもしれない。しかしその光と栄誉は長く輝き続けるだろう。その象徴である花のように、四方からの風に吹き散らされても、武士道はその芳香で人間を祝福し続け、人生を豊かにしてくれるはずだ。長い時を経て、いつか武士道の慣習が葬り去られ、その名が忘れ去られる日がくるとしても、その香りは遠く離れた、見えない丘から漂ってくることだろう。

＊**ゼノン**（前335-前263）　古代ギリシアの哲学者。ストア学派の創始者。

役立つ英語表現 4

【way of thinking】

> The **way of thinking** of a woman is sometimes said to be much different from that of a man. (p.142, 1行目)
> 女性のものの考え方は男性とはずいぶんちがうと言われることがある。

way of thinking は「考え方」のことです。mindset という言い方もよく用いられます。このmindset は20世紀になってから出てきたことばです。

It is hard to work with my immediate boss since his way of thinking is quite different from mine.
私の直属の上司とは考えが異なるので仕事をするのがむずかしい。

I don't understand the mindset of young people.
若者の考え方についていけない。

【climb the ladder】

> The skills of our women were not for show or for **climbing the** social **ladder**. (p.146, 13行目)
> 日本の女性が習い事をするのも、見せびらかしたり、出世したりするためではなかった。

climb the ladderは「階段を上る」というのが直訳ですが、比喩的に用いられることが多く「出世する」ということを意味します。

Mr. Brown was very ambitious and the climbed the corporate ladder to the top in his 40's.
ブラウン氏は非常に野心があり、40代で会社の頂点に立った。

ambitious＝野心のある

【benefit】

> Never, please, never forget the many **benefits** which our good master Hideyori has given you. （p.148, 14行目）
>
> ご主君の秀頼様からの多大なるご恩を決して決してお忘れのないように。

benefitは「恩恵、利益」という意味ですが、ビジネス場面ではfringe benefit(s)という使われ方で「諸手当、恩恵」などを意味する場合が多いです。

> The company offers benefits including insurance, maternity leave, and long summer holidays.
>
> その会社は保険、産休、長期の夏休みなどの福利厚生を提供している。

【in favor of】

> I am not excessively **in favor of** giving up one's own will.
> （p.150, 11行目）
>
> 私は、自分の意志を手放すことを必要以上に持ち上げているわけではない。

in favor of は「〜に賛成する」という意味です。契約書などで、小切手をin favor of the seller で振り出すという場合は「売り手を受取人として」という意味になります。

> The Board was in favor of the merger.
>
> 取締役会は合併に賛成であった。

【in terms of】

> Men are equal only **in terms of** legal rights before the law.
> （p.152, 21行目）
>
> 法律の下での法的な権利だけが平等なのだ。

in terms of「～の観点から」という意味です。他にもin the light of やfrom the standpoint of なども同様に使えます。

> In terms of investment in Asian countries, Japan is far behind.
> アジア諸国への投資という点では、日本はかなり遅れをとっている。

【count】

> As a social-political unit, the woman was not **counted** for much.
> （p.154, 6行目）
> 社会的・政治的な単位としては女性の地位は重くない。

countはまずは単純に「数える」という意味が出てきますが、ここでは「勘定に入れる、重要視する」という意味です。count onで「～を当てにする」という意味で頻繁に使われています。

> I'm counting on your skills.
> あなたのスキル（技術）を頼りにしています。

【regarded as】

> Self-praise is **regarded as** bad taste among us, and I hope among Christian nations also.（p.156, 1行目）
> 日本人の間では、自画自賛は悪趣味とみなされているし、キリスト教徒の間でもそうであってほしいものだ。

regarded as は「～と見なされている」という意味です。

> Nowadays a smart phone is regarded as a business necessity.
> 今やスマートフォンはビジネスの必須アイテムと見なされている。

【pay a price for】

> Unfortunately, there was no gentleman in Eden. Adam and Eve **paid a** high **price for** his absence. （p.158、8行目）
>
> 残念なことに、エデンの園にはジェントルマンは存在しなかった。おかげでアダムとイブは高い代価を払うことになった。

pay a price for は「〜に対して代償を払う」という意味です。pay off と言う表現もよく見かけますが、これは「利益や効果を生む」という意味です。

He had to pay the price for not having prepared for his presentation.
彼はプレゼンの準備を十分に行っていなかったので、高い代償を払うことになった。

Finally her constant effort paid off.
ついに彼女の努力が報われた。

【aggressive】

> Backed by a huge number of reckless working men, these natural-born "bosses" formed a strong check to the **aggressive** rise of the two-sworded class. （p.162、5行目）
>
> 天性の「親分」たちは大多数のむこうみずな労働者の支持を受け、武士階級が過度に台頭しないように目を光らせた。

aggressiveは「積極的」という意味です。文脈にもよりますが、日本語でアグレッシブというと何かネガテイブなイメージがありますが、英語ではむしろ積極的な良いイメージです。

Her aggressive plan was well received among the Board members.
彼女の積極的なプランが取締役たちの間で好評であった。

【exclusive】

We have seen that not one quality of character was **exclusive** to Bushido. （p.166, 12行目）
武士道にしか見られない美点は1つもなかった。

exclusiveは「独占的な、唯一の」という意味です。良い場合でも悪い場合でも極端なイメージがあります。

He was happy to get the exclusive right to sell the product of ABC Corp. in Japan.
彼は日本における ABC 社の独占販売権を得て喜んだ。

exclusive right to sell=独占販売権

【when it comes to...】

But **when it comes to** basic ethical ideas, Bushido is still the guiding light of the transitional period and will prove to be the formative force of new era. （p.168, 14行目）
しかし、基本的な倫理概念として武士道は今も過渡期の日本を導くともし火であり、新しい時代を形づくる力であるのは間違いない。

when it comes to…は「～のことになると、～に関しては」という意味です。

When it comes to making money in the stock market, ask Mr. Brown.
株で儲けることに関してはブラウンさんに聞きなさい。

【defect】

On the other hand, it is fair to recognize that for the faults and
defects of our character, Bushido is also largely responsible.
（p.174, 15行目）
一方、日本人の欠点や短所についても武士道に大きな原因があることを認めねば公平ではないだろう。

defectは「欠陥、不備、不具合」などの意味です。ビジネスの場ではクレームのときによく出てくることばです。人物に関してもコミュニケーションができない人のことをcommunication defectがあると表現することができますが、かなり厳しい言い方です。

Defects were found in the new product and had to be recalled immediately.
新製品に欠陥があることがわかり、すぐに回収された。

【issue】

The problem with the professor became small compared to the moral
issues.（p.176, 22行目）
この道徳的な問いかけを前に、教授をめぐる騒動は些細なものとなった。

issueは「問題」という意味ですが、最近は「イッシュー」などとカタカナ語でも使われ始めています。

Harassment is a sensitive issue in the office now.
ハラスメントはオフィスでは慎重を期する問題である。

【divide】

One wise man said that men have **divided** the world into Christian and non-Christian, without thinking about the good and bad in both.（p.178, 14行目）

ある賢者はこう言った。人々は世界をキリスト教徒と異教徒とに分かち、たがいに善悪を併せ持つことを考えなかった。

divideは動詞では「分ける」という意味で使われることが多いですが、最近は名詞で「格差」を意味することで頻繁に用いられるようになりました。economic divideは「貧富の差」のことを意味します。

Many companies offer training programs to fill the digital divide among the employees.

多くの会社は社員間のデジタル格差をなくすために、様々な研修プログラムを提供している。

【tolerate】

Democracy does not **tolerate** the concentration of power in the hands of only one group.（p.182, 3行目）

民主主義はいかなる特権集団も許さない。

tolerateは「耐える、許容する」という意味です。否定文で用いられることのほうが多いようです。zero toleranceということばも最近頻繁に聞きますが、これは「絶対に許さない、見逃さない」という意味です。

There is zero tolerance for smoking on airplane.

機内での喫煙は絶対に許されない。

English **C**onversational **A**bility **T**est
国際英語会話能力検定

● E-CATとは…
英語が話せるようになるための
テストです。インターネット
ベースで、30分であなたの発
話力をチェックします。

www.ecatexam.com

● iTEP®とは…
世界各国の企業、政府機関、アメリカの大学
300校以上が、英語能力判定テストとして採用。
オンラインによる90分のテストで文法、リー
ディング、リスニング、ライティング、スピー
キングの5技能をスコア化。iTEP®は、留学、就
職、海外赴任などに必要な、世界に通用する英
語力を総合的に評価する画期的なテストです。

www.itepexamjapan.com

［日英対訳］武士道

2021年4月3日　第1刷発行

原著者　　新渡戸稲造

発行者　　浦　　晋　亮

発行所　　**IBCパブリッシング株式会社**
　　　　　〒162-0804 東京都新宿区中里町29番3号 菱秀神楽坂ビル9F
　　　　　Tel. 03-3513-4511　Fax. 03-3513-4512
　　　　　www.ibcpub.co.jp

印刷所　　**株式会社 シナノパブリッシングプレス**

CDプレス　**株式会社 ケーエヌコーポレーションジャパン**

© IBC Publishing, Inc. 2021

Printed in Japan

ISBN978-4-7946-0655-6